Think... Stand-Up..
& Walk Tall

Eliyahu Kelman

ISBN: 978-0-9954776-0-5 (IngramSpark – Hardback)
ISBN: 978-0-9954776-5-0 (IngramSpark – Paperback)
ISBN: 978-0-9954776-1-2 (CreateSpace –Paperback)

A personal message

To the Divine creator and source of everything we have in this world, ideas, blessings, challenges, protection and restriction, for giving me the ideas, opportunities, inspiration, challenges and protection, my wife, my family, friends, neighbours, community, countries and people.

To my dear wife Alice, who stood by me through all my adventures and together with our children and grandchildren acted as a sounding board for the developing ideas and inspiration, finally resulting in the Soul-Secret series.

And with thanks to my close friend and colleague Peter Harris who worked with me during the endless hours we spent pedantically going through the book, again and again. Handling the fine technical and organizational details necessary for this publishing adventure.

*Certainty Absolute Certainty, making the Impossible Possible, **Abra-Ca-Dabra** and the help of the Divine combined together to bring **Think...Stand-Up..& Walk Tall** into reality.*

The Author

Originally an educationalist and school principal, Eliyahu has always retained a thirst for knowledge and understanding; long years of research, delving deeply into the secrets of life, applying this knowledge and understanding as a mentor and guide to countless others.

Eliyahu's career as businessman and entrepreneur has cruised the heights and plumbed the depths as he applied the knowledge within to reach beyond – to prove the impossible possible – taking small opportunities and expanding them beyond all recognition, always agile in successfully responding to the challenges and 'ups and downs' of life, ethical considerations in mind. Eliyahu's philosophy in business life: maximize the upside, minimize the downside; even know when to walk away.

Over the years his fortunes ranged from extremely wealthy, through periods of financial challenge; responding by shrugging his shoulders and brushing himself off, standing up and rebuilding over and over again, never missing a beat. Eliyahu repeatedly created solutions, initiating Joint Ventures and major projects around the world, in a number of sectors both economic and social. He developed innovative solutions, both on his own account and for entities large and small, including for some of the largest global brands and multinational companies. Over time he worked with many high-profile entrepreneurs, businessmen, and political leaders, bringing them solutions and guiding them through times of great change, never standing out in front; always the king-maker, not the king. On occasion this has led to him negotiating in conflict resolution and in the development of core contracts for major banks and corporations, over the course of time he has created and controlled several Public companies.

Eliyahu has led a life of many adventures, living the principles of the Codes of Life, which were slowly accumulated over thousands of years; succeeding almost miraculously in both going through and coming out unscathed.

Making it his life's mission to show others how to change their lives, he has acted as a guide and mentor to thousands.

Table of Contents

'The common eye only sees the outside
of things and judge by that,
but the seeing eye pierces through
and reaches and reads
the heart and the Soul
finding their capacities which
the outside did not indicate or promise,
and which the other kind could not detect'.

Mark Twain 1896

Find Meaning in Life…
and Deepen Relationships

Life is like a mirror,
it reflects what you do
To build good relationships,
you are always number two
Make everyone you deal with,
feel like number one

Don't let your ego get in the way,
it will spoil all the fun

Be humble with your friends,
and everyone you meet
Listen with interest, respect their ideas
Each one is different deep down inside,
all alone with their dreams,
their hopes and their fears,
levels of truth, ambitions and pride
Let everyone win in the great game of life

It's give and take, forget and forgive
Sharing and caring let everyone live

It won't be easy,
the going will be tough
Life is too short,
so there's no going back

Everyone's like an island,
find the right place to land
Then together move forward,
let the relationship expand

Build pleasant memories,
work on it well
This is the key
to make everything jell

Giving and sharing with honor and respect,
serving and leading all with effect

Treat everyone in your life as number one,
modestly accept that you are number two

Remember life is like a mirror
reflecting your thoughts, your actions
straight back on you

Eliyahu Kelman

To find meaning in life, search into the past,
reflect on the differences we made in others' lives

Happiness shared, precious moments that last
The wonders of this world, the places we've seen
all we achieved and what it should mean

Try not to let problems get in the way
Seek meaning through others, what you can give,
We all have a purpose, a reason to live

Embrace all that you are not willing to give up
A person to die for, an impossible dream
Start on the road to find the meaning you seek
keep climbing and climbing, reach up to the peak

Look down to see a stunning sight,
true meaning and friendship
making the world so bright.

Eliyahu Kelman

Introduction

- *An Introduction to the ancient Secrets and Rules*
- *How to internalize them through Spaced-Repetition and Self-Hypnosis*

What is most important of all, it will be you personally, as opposed to other people or situations, taking control of your life for you.

This first book in the Soul Secret series is a step-by-step handbook for everyday living. The ultimate objective is to take you level-by-level, and book-by-book ever deeper into the secrets of life. Embedded within every chapter in this book is the ultimate foundation to find meaning in life, and deepen relationships in so many situations.

You will probably be wondering what kind of experience to expect from a handbook designed to help you find meaning, deepen relationships and handle situations, challenges and the people in your life.

Everyone you meet, from all walks of life, has a Soul. You have a Soul. Your family members have a Soul. A new baby born only seconds ago has a Soul [1]. No matter what religion, creed or color of skin you have, whether you are rich or poor, stupid or clever, you have a Soul. You may ask what is a Soul? How is it relevant to this handbook of life?

Everyone and I mean everyone, puts on a façade – as part of their personality many times during their lifetime.

They hide behind that façade, obscuring their realness and their Soul.

It is interesting to note that the synonyms for the word façade, are face, the outer layer of something; related to 'putting up a front' Etc.

The face that you see is really a façade covering up what is inside the Soul of the person standing in front of you.

With a good part of the world's population, their façade covers up the real character and potential of the Soul lurking under the surface.

> **'Don't walk in front of me;**
> **I may not follow.**
> **Don't walk behind me;**
> **I may not lead.**
> **Just walk beside me and be my friend'.**

Albert Camus and others

As you settle into this book, you will soon realize that the form of the narrative is a 'one-on-one'. with me as your guide. As you read, I want you to imagine that you are really listening to my voice as if I were in the same room with you. The way that I will 'talk' you, through the book will be a different style of English from what you would usually expect in such a book.

The Soul Secret Series is an on-going meditation in the form of Self-Hypnosis, to help you to Internalize the rules and

Secrets embedded within these pages. This unique way of applying a Self-Hypnosis process is really an exercise in **Spaced-Repetition**, repeating everything that you read and learn, again-and-again in your mind. Eventually this will bring about a state of Osmosis.

Repetition is important in everything we do in life, whether it be learning a new dance, studying a new subject, converting our bodies into super fit machines – all these activities and more require repetition. We learn by repetition and Self-Hypnosis and that is something that we must all learn to do.

Spaced-Repetition is in fact a manner of learning, one taught in many schools and universities all over the world. In particular, when learning a new language, one can use the **Spaced-Repetition** method, which will greatly help us, due to the sheer volume of new words to be taken in and retained. If you think about a baby beginning to learn, not only a new language but their first language, the parents will repeat words and actions to them constantly but with spaces or gaps in between. This is a form of **Spaced-Repetition**.

Now, combine that with meditation, which often involves the repeating of a mantra or sound. By repeating certain words, certain phrases and picturing certain images or scenery within your meditation, you are essentially practising **Spaced-Repetition**. This is Self-Hypnosis, available to be used at any time or place when you feel the need to 'walk away' from the pressures of everyday life on the **Default Mode**, as we will refer to it from now on. (See the next chapter for more on the **Default Mode**).

At the end of each chapter, take time to work through what you have learnt so far; repeating over and over again, until all of this becomes a part of your actual being.

The title and book cover were chosen in order to 'drive home' the very strong messages that I feel are necessary and need to be instilled in you; the readers' mind.

Think… Stand-Up.. Walk Tall

And this is exactly what I want you to achieve by the end of the book series.

Everyone is like a tree in the forest[2] with their roots deeply embedded into the ground. What are those roots? They are the DNA of your Soul, together with all of the Souls that are family and friends, or with whom you have interacted in the recent or distant past. The bigger the tree, the deeper the roots and the greater the hidden potential for the Soul to grow and develop, utilizing the gift of 'freedom of choice' for good or bad; success or failure; for creativity; for inventiveness; for building or destruction; and for controversy or calm.

What we see in the forest is the tree, all of its branches and leaves open to the world, but nothing of what is really hidden underneath. Similarly, like the tree, each and every person's mission in life is to grow, flourish and make it to maturity.

That is why we chose the title of this book as **Think… Stand-Up.. & Walk Tall**. Again, it is our intention to achieve just that, a way of thinking, reacting and living, just like the tree in the forest Standing Tall with Certainty – Absolute Certainty.

***The Osmosis
we are all aiming for
is to reach up for the sky
and access all the knowledge
waiting for us on the
Divine Mode***

Eliyahu Kelman

As we move through the chapters, we will be discussing the effects of breathing together. We will see how to sense danger, pleasure, opportunity, solutions and to understand the reality of the people we interact with on a day-to-day basis.

You will find many powerful secrets that will open up and reveal that which is hidden inside the forest and these will help you to reach down to the real roots of life.

Finally, we come to the 'background music' of everything written in this book. The very secret for deepening the connection and commitment between you and the people you are dealing with.

This is one of the most powerful secret tools that you can take into your life. Look around you. Don't you find that this is really the key to all relationships, commitments, friendships, loyalties and beliefs in society? You see its effect in schools, universities, the military, hospitals and in many other places where people congregate.

'Those who Breathe Together
Bond and Stay Together'

We have a lot of work to do on this voyage of discovery. This is the reason why I am recommending that you try to keep me in your minds-eye and imagine the echo of my voice, whilst I am taking you through this journey, with all of the challenges and pleasures that will lead us to the ultimate destination of each person and every Soul.

Interwoven within the coming chapters are real-life stories, sometimes quite fantastical and living proof of the Rules and Secrets in action. Every time I dig into those memories, I think to myself 'I would never have believed that this really happened, had I not been there myself'.

The short stories and ditties
spread throughout the book
are Spaced-Repetition
with hypnosis inside
To help Internalize and change your life
repeat each message again and again,
osmosis will happen
through the power of my pen

A symphony of sound
coming down through the ages
ever streaming into our minds

As we turn the pages
the music plays
and our destiny we find
the story of our life from Default to Divine
ancient secrets revealed
our lives we refine

Reach up, reach up to the sky
Walking Tall, with our Souls
upwards we fly

Eliyahu Kelman

Trees stand tall
and so should you
Reaching up to the sky
in the direction they grew
Take control of your life,
stand firm, stand strong
Realise your power,
you can't go wrong
Believe In yourself
know who you are
Be sure be strong,
just follow the secrets,
you'll never go wrong

Eliyahu Kelman

A unique STAND UP MEDITATION

Think… Stand-Up.. & Walk Tall

- *Let me introduce you to our unique approach to meditation and Self-Hypnosis, by having our first short meditation together.*

- *Reach beyond yourself - Whenever you need courage; a boost to face up to tragedy or challenge, a task towering beyond your reach.*

- *This is the time to get your Adrenaline running and to draw down the energy from the Divine.*

Just Stand-Up and Meditate

Concentrate on the picture on the cover of this book, which is a quiet peaceful forest out in the countryside. You can feel, hear, and almost touch the silence. Now **Stand-Up**, close your eyes, and imagine that you are one of the trees out there in our very private forest. Why do we use the image of you as a tree, surrounded by other trees? Trees 'Stand Tall'. forever reaching up to the sky and to the limitless space above the tops of their branches.

Now start swaying slowly back and forth, just like a tree in the wind. Pull your head back and push your mind higher and higher. Hold this position for a few minutes.

With concentration, you will actually start to feel the force of your Soul and mind standing 'taller and taller'.

In the beginning, you will find it difficult to hold the 'upward' movement and will feel your mind slipping down. Keep focusing on the space high up above your head and concentrate on just pushing up. Repeating this exercise through **Spaced-Repetition**, you will gradually and automatically move up to this mode on demand.

Start swaying back and forth, back and forth ever so slowly like a tree in the wind. This will help you to connect with your Soul. Now you are ready to start drawing down energy from the Divine Mode. Open the palms of your hands and stretch them out from the sides of your body, with your palms facing upwards, ready to receive the energy forces generated from the Divine level.

Concentrate on receiving the energy and feel your hands start to get warmer. With complete concentration on the upward movement, the swaying, and receiving the downloaded energy into the palm of your hands, you will uplift your Soul towards the Divine Mode.

Let us repeat this exercise after relaxing for a few moments. This is our first step towards defragging and re-programming your mind. **Spaced-Repetition** will serve as the very foundation on which the Self-Hypnosis and meditation exercises will be built into future chapters.

This exercise is different from most of the systems of meditation that many of our readers will have been practising for years. I want to encourage you to continue with the form of meditation to which you have grown accustomed. This will help you think and Internalize the messages that are being conveyed and highlighted in the Secrets and Rules, summed up in the different forms of Mantras'. centred on individual pages throughout the book.

The purpose of the Soul Secret series is to change your life, and of those close to you, linking up to the Divine Mode and enjoying all of its benefits. You need to delve into the secrets and rules in order to help you to move up to that level.

Meditation is an important tool that will help you to do just that.

Continuously repeat this exercise again and again, both throughout the book and in your daily lives. In addition to the other meditations, this will help you to reach the goals in life that we have set for ourselves.

Trigger this off through '**Spaced-Repetition**' and by repeating this special exercise again and again you will gradually open up the channels[3] from your mind to the 'Big Brain' activating a continuous flow of downloaded messages. Repeated swaying back and forth, back and forth will help you to connect your mind to your Soul.

You are downloading the energy generated from the Divine Mode through the palms of your hands so fuelling a 'lift off' from the Default to the Divine. Standing Tall with your head back and pushing your mind ever upwards will generate a feeling of certainty and confidence.

Swaying back and forth whilst reading, studying, researching and problem solving has a powerful effect on your ability to connect your mind and your Soul to whatever the subject you are handling at that moment.

Whenever I research or study, I get a feeling of clarity and a deeper understanding if just I remember to keep on swaying.

Try it whilst reading this book.

Man is like a tree [2], *with the mighty trunk of intellect, the spreading branches of imagination, and the roots of the lower instincts that bind him to the earth*
The moral life, however, is the fruit he bears; in it his true nature is revealed.

Felix Adler

'There is a vitality,
a life force, an energy,
a quickening that is translated through
you into action, and because there is
only one of you in all of time, this expression
is unique. And if you block it, it will never
exist through any other medium and it
will be lost. The world will not have it.
It is not your business to determine how
good it is nor how valuable nor how
it compares with other expressions.
It is your business to keep it yours clearly
and directly, to keep the channel open.
You do not even have to believe
in yourself or your work.
You have to keep yourself open and aware
to the urges that motivate you.
Keep the channel open'.

Martha Graham

Chapter One

The Hidden World We Live In

- *Wouldn't it be a dream if everyone came with a handbook?*

- *Learning to download, streaming messages from the Big Brain*

- *Getting to the 'Source Code'*

Before you settle into this book, I want to welcome you to an entirely new experience in your life. It is important to bear in mind that all of the Secrets and Rules are drawn from the ancient writings of the Sages, going way back to the beginning of time

The real life experience stories interwoven throughout this book, will illustrate how the hidden rules and secrets in the handbook for life really work. This, together with a new form of meditation to help you to Internalize everything you learn. As mentioned, the meditation is a Self-Hypnosis process, a repetition of what you read and ultimately what you hear in your Soul.

A few words again, about the title of the book ...

Think...
Stand Up..
& Walk Tall

The whole purpose of this book is to do exactly that.

The way you think has to become the automatic way you act. When you do not know what to do, you are generally advised to **Stand-Up** – go forward and take action. 'Walk Tall' is the ultimate target. Believe in what you do with such certainty that you will constantly reach for the sky as do the trees in the forest on the cover of this book.

Constantly keep this in your mind, internalise it, think it through carefully, develop your own thoughts then act. **Stand-Up** to be counted, Walk Tall.

The way we act can sometimes be the problem. Yes, we can think before we stand and before we walk, but it is what we think that determines how we will stand and walk and in turn, what we will say and do. We will work on all of this as we progress through the book together.

I want you to imagine that we are here together for a personal chat where we will tell each other from the inside how we feel. This is a rare opportunity to communicate and just think. Take advantage of this opportunity.

Think about this for a moment. Why do people go to Facebook, Twitter or any of the other social media platforms? They want to tell their story, to be treated like individuals and human beings. They reach out with a part of their Soul in the hope that someone else will reach back to them.

Nobody, in this world, is like a Pinocchio, where everybody comes out of a factory, a clone of each other. Each person wants to be recognised as an individual, a unique Soul.

Each and every person is a delicately balanced instrument, deserving of being recognised as such. We should be treating people the same way we want people to treat us.

Why do I start off this way? Because every one of us realises that we're living in a world full of chaos. We are surrounded by chaos, chaos in our personal lives, in our business lives and everything in between. Future historians will look back and call these times the 'Era of Chaos' [4].

You can't trust Banks, you can't trust governments, you can't even trust your own security and in many cases, even those pretty close to you. But, we all have that choice to reach out and strive to live above the chaos on a different level.

There is so much that we do not understand. This makes life's decision-making processes very difficult and confusing. This book is about making a change, helping you to take back control of your life, your mind, your Soul and your future.

We all have day-to-day challenges, each and every one of us.

Wouldn't it be a dream if each and every person would came with a handbook? Just think about all of the equipment you use every single day at home, at work and in your car. These could be your computer, your mobile and, all the paraphernalia of a modern life in a connected world. Without a handbook or step-by-step guide, you'll probably not get the most advantage out of the item and perhaps even spoil what you bought. If we all came with a handbook, life could be very different - but we don't, and this is the problem.

Wouldn't it be a dream if the people we deal with on a day-to-day basis all came with a handbook?

If only we had a handbook showing us in great detail how to handle them - and them us, what a different world we would live in. We could, essentially, meet someone and say, 'I would like to get to know how to be with you. Please hand over your handbook so I can start to learn all about how you function and how I should treat you'. Or when faced with a troublesome situation, we simply pull out the handbook of life and look up, say 'How to negotiate an amicable outcome between myself and my wife with regards to a matter we disagree with. What to do when tragedy hits, possibly a death or serious illness, bankruptcy, losing your job, your house, your spouse, best friend and so many other challenges in life'.

Imagine the possibilities!

Soul Secrets is all about learning how to access the handbook of everyone and everything in our lives.

For more than 30 years, I have researched into the meaning of life, the hidden keys to living and achieving the ultimate. During my studies I've sought out and read thousands of sources, commentaries and ancient books, some of them going back even to the beginning of time.

In my years of reading and research, I have learnt that the Sages knew the secrets of the world, how the world operated and how we interface with everything around us, with nature, with birds, fish, other animals, and human beings.

I'm going to show you a bit later how much they knew. Ironically, they knew most of what the scientists have only discovered in recent years. But we'll talk about that later.

As mentioned earlier on, Self-Hypnosis plays an important role in this process. In order to succeed we have to imagine and picture in our mind's eye an image, a vision of what we want to do and where we want to be.

To have success in this process we must close our eyes and envisage that situation, whether it be a happy marriage, a happy relationship with our children, success in our workplace or having money in the Bank, whichever we want.

To attain success in your career and live a meaningful life, you have to meditate and visualize. This Book will do just that. You will find this different and dynamic. Go over each chapter again and again, really Internalizing and making this a part of you in your new personality. And by new personality, I mean the person you are meant to be, the person slowly starting to surface as you work your way through this wonderful journey with me.

Now, what we need to do is to Internalize this experience, while separating our Soul from our body and really seeing a difference between the Soul and our physical being.

The brain comes with very sophisticated software, just like a computer. You've got the hardware, your body, so that's not a problem. The software, however, while installed, is not completely activated.

I'm going to show you how to activate that software and help you to open up the channels to the Big Brain. The Big Brain is all that surrounds us, all the space, all the unseen connections. You will be able to connect to the channels[3] for life and download messages into your mind.

In order to experience this, I want you to close your inner eyes (the eyes of your Soul) and while reading, imagine that we are taking our Souls up for a journey into space. It will help if you to go to my website at www.Soulsecret.com and watch the two minute Video a number of times. Then come back to this meditation and hold the picture in your mind.

Now, here we are up in space. Let's turn around and look back at the Earth. How different it looks on this level. What do you see through your Soul? Just look. We are above time, space and motion[5].

What a wonderful feeling… right? Down on Earth we are attached to time, space and motion. It's confusing and difficult, and we continuously chase after ourselves. Up here in space, it is entirely different.

Now, let us take a few seconds to think about our Soul.

Everybody has a Soul [1]
There is no such thing on the Soul level
as Race, Creed, Gender, Rich, Poor,
Tall or Short, Smart or Stupid

Eliyahu Kelman

The Soul doesn't have any of that because a Soul is all of the positive things that I just mentioned now, none of the negative.

To what extent do we understand what this is all about? The Soul has the built in software. The Soul is your operating system, the core platform required to run your body, to control and direct the hidden recesses of your mind. Once we assume control, sitting firmly in the driver's seat, you see the whole world change and feel different, entering a new reality, a radically richer and deeper perspective.

A movie comes to mind, you may have watched it in awe, thinking that it was just movie mumbo jumbo. 'Lucy'; this is the story of a woman who succeeded in ingesting a unique chemical composition, enabling her to access every last bit of her brainpower. Lucy realised, as will you as you progress on this journey with me, that you and many others in this world, are living on a **Default Mode**. The majority of the general population, in fact, are utilising perhaps 10% of their brainpower, maybe even less. This, in itself, is sad. To think, we have all this greatness, but don't ever access it. What a waste!

Let's think of how we all live back on earth, in our physical environment, in the world of chaos that we have left behind on the...

Default Mode

Why? Because when you switch on your computer, and haven't yet activated the software, your computer will automatically operate on 'default' according to the way it was set up in the factory.

Up here, in space, we are on the …

Divine Mode

At any point in time, we can always escape up to this level and look down at the chaos. All of the secrets, rules, meditation and Internalization are here to help us to reach a level that will enable us to live on the Divine Mode whilst working through our lives on the **Default Mode**.

In the reality of the world we're living in, credibility is very important. We must not leave any doubt in your mind that you can clearly trust the secrets and the mentors who deliver and explain.

I want to give you a few facts that will help you to accept that the ancients had a deep and fundamental understanding of how the Universe works, so that you can work through this book, start on this journey with complete confidence and know that all I am giving you is credible.

The first example… The Stars…

When you have a chance, just have a look out there. In some parts of the world, the stars are more visible than in others, but they are still there, myriads and myriads of stars and planets, seemingly going on forever.

Do you have any idea how many are out there? Well, NASA now says that there are trillions upon trillions of stars in the universe – at this moment they calculate some 10 to the power of 25, but who knows…

Bear in mind that astronomers made use of the Hubble telescope together with very sophisticated computers and software in order to arrive at these figures.

Do you know what happened in ancient times, a few thousand years ago in the days of the Talmud?[5] The Sages (the wisest of men) gave us a detailed calculation of how many stars and planets can be found in space. Remember that this was at a time when the ancients believed that there were only four thousand stars, planets and other celestial bodies in the galaxy.

The Sages expressed their calculation using the military terms of the time and as later used by the armies of Rome...

- 12 Constellations of the zodiac.

- each of 30 Armies;

- each of 30 Legions;

- each of 30 Divisions;

- each of 30 Cohorts;

- each of 30 Camps;

- each of 365 Myriads

- each of 10,000 Soldiers

(In ancient times, a myriad was generally held to be a unit of 10,000)

Think: 365 x 10,000 x 12 x 30 x 30 x 30 x 30 x 30 x 2

This ancient calculation[6] by the Sages resolves as 2×10^{15}.

Taking into consideration that those very same scientists and Sages told us that the universe is expanding with time and because it is expanding, we actually reached a relatively similar figure.

Remember, that the Sages didn't have any of the equipment that the scientists have today. To take this even further, Black Holes[7] are mentioned and described in the Zohar, an ancient Kabbalistic text.

We can go even further than that when we discuss the String Theory (a theory on the fundamental structure and operation of the universe) and the 10 dimensions (discussed a little bit later). For many years these theories have been the subject of an ongoing argument between scientists; a few years back a team of Japanese scientists postulated that there are actually 10 dimensions on the physical level.

It should be noted that there are multiple sets of the ten dimensions known as 'The 10 Emanations - Eser Sfirot'. Some of these will be discussed in the more advanced books in the series as we move up onto the Divine Mode.

It may surprise you that the ancients knew that there were 10 dimensions. To go all the way back to the time of Abraham, a little over four thousand years ago, Abraham wrote in 'The Book of Creation'[8] all of the calculations on how the universe worked, including an in-depth description of the 10 dimensions.

The 10 dimensions, according to the scientists, are what filter our gravity so that we can move about in the manner we do.

Now for a little explanation - a 101 on the 10 dimensions. The 10 dimensions are made up of certain aspects; the first three are the ones that we understand and use in everyday life, length, height and depth. The fourth dimension is time.

The fifth and sixth dimensions are all about the merging of worlds, others and ours in the universe. The seventh dimension is also about other possible worlds, where the conditions are different to ours. The eighth dimension starts to become a little complicated to explain, but basically involves the infinities of universe histories. The ninth dimension allows us to compare all the possible laws of physics with the very first conditions that existed. The final dimension is where it would be possible to do and be anything and everything.

As you can see, we are very far from reaching the tenth dimension, never mind the fourth.

Let me explain what this really means, why it is so important, and why we had to discuss the subject. It is necessary to understand that the force is strongest at its source, its energy so powerful that if the surface of the earth were bombarded with its full force, any life would be impossible.

Scientists worked out, as had the ancients, that out in space the force of gravity is too strong to create an environment that would support life, as we know it today.

Space scientists use gravity-assist to speed spacecraft, sling-shotting them between planets, even out to interstellar space and beyond the gravitational pull of our sun, exploiting gravity to minimize or eliminate the need to burn scarce fuel. Gravity is so powerful that if it wasn't filtered down through the 10 dimensions to the surface of the Earth, what life would we be able to live?

Consider this for a moment. If the force of gravity were just a little bit stronger, we would find it difficult to walk. Our feet would be stuck to the ground. Cars wouldn't be able to move. We wouldn't be able to exist. And if it were a little bit weaker, what would happen? We would be floating above the earth and wheels wouldn't be turning. Nothing would function properly or as we know it to function today.

So, it's because of those exact filters, finely tuned at the time that the world was created, as was known by the ancients' way back then, we are able to function as we do today.

It is not just great ideas that are made up from people's experiences in life. No. The incredible stories I am going to bring you are about how life works in practice.

The beginnings of the Universe, from the time of the first explosion and how space then expanded from nothing, is described in very great detail in Kabbalistic writings. So, if we just take those few examples, which give credibility on the scientific level, then we will realise that everything else can be believed as well. However what we're talking about is beyond the reach of science. This is the inner space that is in our minds and linked to our Souls. Science has no way of discovering and proving what is going on deep inside our minds and connecting through our Soul.

Now, I want you to imagine a group of scientists climbing a very high mountain in their quest to discover ultimate truth. Parts of that journey we already know.

When they were first studying DNA, they were also experimenting with the idea of cloning animals in laboratories, and if the law would ever allow it, they would attempt to reproduce human beings in the same way. They all had one major problem.

Just imagine if after a long climb up the mountain, they finally managed to open the door to their 'Eureka moment'. They would be convinced that they had uncovered the truth in their own reality of existence, without a Divine architect behind it all. They suddenly would see the image of G-d smiling at them and simply stating, 'Aa ha, but I have the source code'[9].

> *'I believe in the inalienable*
> *right of all adult scientists*
> *to make absolute fools*
> *of themselves in private'*

Sydney Brenner

Sydney Brenner was one of the four leading scientists who organised the Asilomar conference, at which the key resolution describing and now controlling the principles of research into the manipulation of Genes was presented. This resolution was adopted unanimously by the scientific and lay delegates present.

This is exactly what we're talking about - The **Source Code**[9].

The very source of all information is what we are going to learn about and how to harness it, as I take you through this incredible journey.

An important fact to bear in mind, when developing our thinking, will be the role the human brain plays in all of this. As we discussed earlier, there is the relationship between the Big Brain and our Brain and connecting through the Soul.

We are going to take a look at what the ancient scientists told us about the truth of the world. If we just calculate how many Glial cells, synapses, and connectors there are in the brain, it will come very close to the figure that NASA gave us for the Universe.

Almost the same as the Talmud gave us for the stars and planets in the universe.

It's incredible. Just think of this amazing and sad fact. All of us are working and walking around with this sophisticated equipment, and we haven't even downloaded and activated most of the software, if any at all.

It is also sad to realise that almost everybody is living on the **Default Mode**, underutilizing their potential and capabilities.

Now, once we understand that we are dealing with a Soul and the Divine is the 'Big Soul', we realise that, likewise brain has the same make up, in miniature, of the BIG BRAIN. We can then look at everything from an entirely different perspective.

Just look how important it is to download all the software, activate the programming and link to the Big Brain as soon as possible. Then and only then will you be able to get that streaming information flowing into your brain all of the time. It is a lot of work, it is not easy, and we have to take this step-by-step, in order for us to understand much more, as to where we are going and the place we want to be.

Before moving on, we need to understand this important rule

Let your family participate…
All problems and challenges
becoming a joint effort
and responsibility
Be open and frank,
seek out solutions,
unity is strength
Give mutual support
Combat 'Brain-Pollution'

Eliyahu Kelman

Every Soul
is likened to a Universe [10]
When you hurt a person,
you hurt a Universe
When you damage a person,
you damage a Universe
And when you kill a person,
you destroy a Universe
and any other new Universes
that could have been born
through that person
in their future world

Eliyahu Kelman

Now, once we understand that we are dealing with a Soul and the Divine is the 'Big Soul', we realise that, likewise that the brain has the same make up, in miniature, as the BIG BRAIN. We can then look at everything from an entirely different perspective.

Just look how important it is to download all the software, activate the programming and link to the Big Brain as soon as possible. Then and only then will you be able to get that streaming information flowing into your brain all of the time. It is a lot of work, it is not easy, and we have to take this step-by-step, in order for us to understand much more, as to where we are going and the place we want to be.

We need to go deeper into the truth of the world. That is what The Soul Secret Series is all about. This is the real source for taking control of your life.

Are you ready?

'The Soul
is placed in the body
like a rough diamond,
and must be polished,
or the lustre of it
will never
appear'

Daniele Defoe

Chapter Two

Your Body – The Spacesuit of your Soul[11]

- *What is a soul - how to connect*

There is an important question that we need to ask ourselves before we go deeper into this voyage of discovery.

Everyone wants to succeed...
How sincere are you?
Are you willing to put in the effort
to bring about success?

This investment in yourself is small. The effort is concentrated into continuous meditation and relaxation.

Do you know when you should be meditating or 'self-hypnotising?' You should do it when things are tense, or during a challenge in your life, or when you don't know how to handle something. This is the time to close yourself off in your room, before relaxing in an easy chair and going into your 'inner space'.

Go back to the 'Stand-Up Meditation'
on page 10.

Take yourself into another world way up into outer space, on the level of your Soul, and if each and every time you have a challenge, you do just that, then gradually you will find it easier to leave the **Default Mode** behind and go up onto the Divine Mode.

Now, let us move forward.

I mentioned before about spacesuits. The human spacesuit has four portals and five senses: eyes to see, ears to hear, mouth to speak, nose to breathe and to smell. And with all these senses, the only one, which is really on the Divine Mode, is the sense of smell.

The Eyes

We must try to control what we see and what we look at. We ultimately choose what we look at. But, sometimes something flashes into our vision and we can't help but look at it. We have no control and it has an effect on us. So, we have to be very, very careful as to what we allow our eyes to see. This is an important rule to remember in this process.

> *'You can't depend on the eyes;*
> *When your imagination is out of focus'*

Mark Twain 1887

It's dangerous, for all sorts of reasons and situations.

> *Don't allow your Heart and*
> *Mind to follow your Eyes* (12)

38

The Ears

With your ears, you can control what you're going to listen to. Maybe you will choose a beautiful symphony; or decide that this time you're going to listen to your wife, your husband or your partner; or even possibly end up listening to a lecture. There are so many ways where you have control, one is making the decision as to what you allow yourself to hear, as much can enter your hearing range. You need to learn when it's the right time to switch off. You control the switch

> *'G-d gave us two ears and one mouth,*
> *So we ought to listen*
> *twice as much as we speak'*

The Mouth

This is the portal through which we speak. Speaking is both powerful and dangerous; the world was created by words. The Ten Commandments were given in the right combination of words. Words can be so powerful that we must try to measure and carefully calculate what we say. Words can destroy and words can build. Words can encourage and words can discourage.

Once words are out in the open, it is the words that are all powerful, so we have to be careful what we say.

'Words are seeds
that do more than blow around
They land in our hearts
and not on the ground
Be careful what you plant
and careful what you say
You might have to eat what
you planted one day'

Anon

The ancient Sages tell us the reason why our tongue is locked inside such a strong room. It has teeth to stop it from exiting, lips to enclose it. And when used properly, the strong room won't let anything out. So, gritting your teeth is often the smartest way to go. Be aware of what you say, or don't say if at all.

Let us consider a few situations together. When you are at a meeting, no matter on what level it is. It could be at a Board of Directors meeting, the parents meeting of your children's school or possibly a public forum. Sometimes you see someone there who listens but doesn't talk, seemingly just sitting there and thinking. You don't know if he is a wise man or not, but many would think he is a very wise person, and he is, in a way. Sometimes only speaking when you have something really relevant to say is the best time to speak. Many speak and actually never say anything at all.

But, there are also times when you need to speak up. There are times in life that you have to speak up. There are times in life where somebody tries to abuse you and you have to tell them straight how you feel about it or tell them to stop.

When we don't say what needs to be said, or on the flipside, when we say things that are wrong, hurtful or meaningless, we are communicating with words in the language of the **Default Mode**. The danger is that it can destroy everything on the **Divine Mode**[13].

The Nose

In our human spacesuit, we have a portal, used for breathing and for the sense of smell, functions we can't live without. The ancient word to breathe 'linshom'. shares the same root as the Hebrew word for Soul 'Neshamah'.

41

Even those who do not understand these Hebrew words can recognise that the two sounds are similar.

In fact, they are more alike than just in sound. A soul and a breath are almost the same. In the Old Testament, we are told that when Adam[14], meaning 'man' was formed, G-d breathed the breath of life[15] into man. What was he actually doing? He was breathing the Divine Soul into Adam through the very same portal. So, it stands to reason that we all have a part of that Divine Soul inside of us, as we all come from Adam. Now that we know this, we should understand that every breath we take is very powerful. Every breath will not only keep us alive, but also keep the Soul functioning.

We have dealt with the four portals of the human spacesuit but only one sense is left, and that is the sense of smell, a sense of the Divine. The ability to smell is subliminal, but with your radar up and on the Divine Mode, you will be able to sense the messages being conveyed in real time, both negative and positive.

Aside from sensing the natural smells in life, when you have developed this sense to a higher degree you will actually be able to smell the atmosphere around people and situations, such as love, friendship, tension and fear. It is significant that animals are able to use these higher sensibilities, or 'scentabilities', and there is no reason why we shouldn't be able to do so too. After all, we are a level above the animal world, are we not?

We have all used expressions such as 'this doesn't smell right' or 'I like the smell of that'. Your sense of smell can warn you about so much, such as whether a food has turned and is rotten, whether someone has been in a room by their perfume that still lingers and if food cooking is burning. But it is the finer and higher developments of smell that we need to learn still.

When I was in the banking industry, I would use the bankers smell test in so many situations. Bankers are able to smell out whether a situation is good or bad. When it comes to working with money, this skill is very important and very apt. For me it never proved wrong, unless I chose not to take the sensation seriously. This, not taking a sensation seriously, is also part of the Message system, which we will go into in more detail later on in the book. Sometimes I made the mistake of thinking I could handle the negative aspect of the smell test messages[16].

But, let us move on.

Having covered the physical side of our human spacesuit, imagine that we are looking through the 'sight portal'. seeing the people around us. Take notice that we are seeing the world at 180-degrees, with everyone limited to their individual spacesuit. However, we should bear in mind that others too have a 180-degree view of the world and they, too, view us as being limited by our spacesuits.

Let us think about the times when we looked at somebody, were we seeing their reality as they really were? Now go to a mirror, or better still take look at someone else. You are seeing the spacesuit, not the person, because the person is the Soul.

This is the reason that people acquire unjustified, inflated egos and feelings of superiority. Let us reflect on what we are actually seeing. We see, it seems, that everyone else is limited in their own body, but we do not seem to be limited at all.

Whatever we see in the world around us is subjective. How we interpret something will be different to how another interprets it. Similarly, there is no situation where we see or hear the same way as another person. Everyday people report accidents, robberies, crimes or even miracles in their own unique way, as they perceive it. One can take a little test, where we are shown a video clip of a robbery taking place. Afterwards, we are asked to answer a few questions around the scene we have just witnessed. Many get the answers wrong, such as 'what color was the robber's shirt?' or 'which direction did the robber run?' It is not only our perception of details and scenarios that will differ from one person to another, but also how we interpreted the various segments of the scene. How to accurately recall something we have seen is a skill worth cultivating.

Let us consider Einstein's Theory of Relativity. Relativity is inherent in the way we think, react and assess any situation.

If we look at our inner space, our own personality and character, the way we see ourselves, and the way others see us, it can be best described as the reflection of ourselves as seen in a mirror.

Have you noticed that when you lift up your right hand, your reflected image actually lifts up its left hand? Likewise, when you lift your left hand the image shows the right being raised.

Surely we want to be seen as we really are, but it doesn't always work that way. If I walk towards a mirror, I see my reflection walking towards me. So, in fact we are really walking from opposite directions, coming towards a meeting point somewhere in the middle.

Why am I comparing my mirror image as the difference between the real me and my image as, perceived by others?

The answer is on the level of the Divine Mode, where we learn how to relate to an awareness of our true selves, and that of others.

*What is
important
is to project
your true image,
and always to be aware
of the inner reflective image
of other people*

Here is an important rule and a necessary awareness.

Beware, Be-aware
Beware of yourself
Beware of others...
Reflect your true self
Remove the façade

Show that you
are what's really inside
People are just a reflection
in a world of mirrors they hide,
Be aware, Be-aware
Beware the illusion
that cannot abide

Eliyahu Kelman

When you find fault in someone else,
it is revealing a fault in you
If you don't like something that
somebody else is doing,
check within yourself first
You will usually find the same
fault in you
When you point a finger at me,
just look at what you are hiding
beneath your hand
Three accusing fingers are pointing
back at you...[17]

Eliyahu Kelman

That's how we all behave. That's why we recognise fault in others. Conjure up this picture in your mind

Now is the time to make sure that we are perfectly relaxed and ready to Internalize what we have learned today. It was powerful. It was all empowering.

We learned about the brain, and how remarkable it is that we and everyone around us are compared to a whole universe, nothing more and nothing less.

We learnt that we are a carbon copy of the Big Brain, but a miniature version. We learnt that we are at one with the animals, birds and fish in the sea, the plants, trees and other vegetation, because everything on this level has the root of the Soul. All living things have a Soul on the level of the 'life force'. also known as 'nefesh'. in Hebrew.

Let us reflect together on how we can relate to what we have learnt and the way we are living our lives. We need to inject into our minds a determination to lift ourselves up to the Divine Mode by implementing everything we have learnt so far, just like the mirror image scenario.

We need to keep reflecting on the differences between what we really are and the person we would like to be. In the Divine Mode you can be that person. Just imagine all of the benefits that will become available on the Divine Mode. By continuous Self-Hypnosis and meditation, you will be able to take yourself into the Divine Mode. Remember, this is the exam of your life, the exam for your life. This is the only way you are going to pass and win your entry to the Divine Mode.

Just Stand-Up and Meditate

Concentrate on the cover picture of this book, a quiet peaceful forest far from the city. You can feel, hear, and almost touch the silence. Now **Stand-Up**, close your eyes, and imagine that you are one of the trees out there in our very private forest.

Now...! Start swaying slowly back and forth, just like a tree in the wind. Pull your head back and push your mind higher and higher. Hold this position for a few minutes. With concentration, you will actually start to feel the force of your Soul and mind standing 'taller and taller'.

In the beginning, you will find it difficult to hold the 'upward' movement and will feel your mind slipping down. Keep focusing on the space high up above your head and concentrate on just pushing up.

Sway back and forth, back and forth ever so slowly like a tree in the wind. This will help you to connect with your Soul. Now start drawing down energy from the Divine Mode. Open your hands, palms upwards, stretching out from the sides of your body. Receive the energy forces generated from the Divine.

Concentrate on receiving the energy , feel your hands starting to get warmer. Concentrating on the upward movement, the swaying, and receive the downloaded energy into the palms of your hands.

Repeat this exercise...

Reach up, reach up
above the chaos in your life
Leave behind the confusion and strife,
striving to reach ever greater heights
Keep the Divine Mode ever in sight,
a parallel world all in your mind
Rid of Brain-Pollution, peace you will find
Be certain and sure that you will succeed,
Spaced-Repetition is all that you need
Just reach, reach up
and in Certainty believe

Eliyahu Kelman

Chapter Three

The House with a 360 Degree View

- *More about self-hypnosis*

- *Living above the chaos that surrounds us*

- *How to sail through life, separating ourselves from brain pollution*

Welcome to Chapter Three where we will take you to the first level of the Divine Mode.

All of us were pre-programmed, before we were born, each of us came with individual factory settings. We describe this as the **Default Mode**. Our task in life is to lift ourselves up higher and higher, activating the built-in software as we go.

The Divine Mode is divided into two levels, the intellectual and the spiritual. We are able to activate the higher intellectual level with the powerful energy force of the Divine.

Many people seem to have split personalities. And I don't mean this in a negative way at all. In fact, it is a good thing. They are running on the **Default Mode**, as we all do, when they suddenly start to receive inspiration, becoming creative, motivated, positive, happy, and so on. They suddenly have an emotional feeling. It could be during a prayer, or while interacting with their children, their family, a friend, the outside world, during a concert, or while looking at a painting or landscape, even when fishing or on a sea voyage.

It could happen at any time. We just need to understand what it is all about.

Sometimes we feel connected, we feel good and often inspired. But, most of the time we don't even notice what is surrounding us, including our family and friends, or even our Spouse. Because, most of us are still living within our inner space, attempting to react to the outside world and then slipping back within ourselves, to our own inner body. This is normal, well, as normal as we know it. But it needn't be like this all the time.

Yes, it is difficult to keep on that Divine Mode all of the time, so we try to do as much as we can to keep going back.

Now we continue the Self-Hypnosis concept of meditating on everything we have covered so far. This is an important part of the process. Please don't skip it.

Every day we are used to taking in so much information, we get so confused that we go into 'overload' and give up on trying to understand. We think that we're listening, but most times we are just hearing. We haven't absorbed the true meaning behind the words. Thinking on the **Default Mode** is easy. On the Divine Mode it is altogether different. There is much that we must absorb; a whole new learning process to be learnt; a new way; another approach and a different way of looking at things. Do not be concerned if it is not working out the first time.

Remember this important message:

Internalize
through Spaced-Repetition
until osmosis takes place
and then whatever you learn
will become a part of the inner you
Essentially this is Self-Hypnosis
through Spaced-Repetition,
repeating again and again
the lessons and secrets,
poems and advice
Stand-Up meditation
again and again will never suffice

Think on this…

To become a doctor, learn to speak a new language or to play and understand music or poetry requires repetition. We don't suddenly wake up one morning and find that we can, after one lesson, know how to do all of this. In the beginning, we all stumble and struggle, but **Spaced-Repetition** is the bridge that leads us to eventual osmosis.

Some people take longer whilst others have to make more of an effort. The key to this process is patience. Never try to rush the process. This series has been carefully structured to make sure that we move forward at the right pace. Allow us to lead the way for you.

I want to describe this process to you in a very beautiful way. I want you to imagine you are living the centre of a busy town. You occupy a downstairs apartment, living within a small world of your own… outside your apartment a crowded, noisy street. As soon as you step out of your front door, the world greets you with a cacophony of sound, thousands of people walking by, preoccupied by their busy lives; the bustle of traffic and speeding vehicles, all oblivious to the world around them. Of course, there is pollution as well, environmental, sound, light, water and even visual pollution.

The most difficult challenge of all is Brain-Pollution, of which there is an enormous amount

So many people live in the rat race of life; it is a hard life with no hope of ever changing, unless you make it happen from within.

Living in the rat race is living on the **Default Mode**. We all have to get up early in the morning, eat a quick breakfast or not bother to eat at all. We dash around, working against time, off to work, to catch a bus or train, taking the car and struggling to find parking. We work all day, most times for someone else. At the end of the day you might go for a drink or coffee with your friends or colleagues, all running through life without stopping to think.

How on earth can people manage to escape the **Default Mode** and get out of the rut that they are in? They can't seem to change their lives, until something suddenly hits them.

They could lose their job; go bankrupt or the Bank forecloses. Their wife or husband could suddenly leave them, cheat on them or no longer be loyal. Maybe a sudden tragedy hits, somebody close dies or becomes seriously ill, it could be you. Everything is turned upside down and thrown out of sync.

For most people, these events would be life shattering - why life shattering? Because we are all used to routine, human beings are routine beings. We thrive on routine, in fact. We are creatures of habit and although our routine can be quite complicated at times, quite involved, but still routines.

Whether you are the President or CEO of an international company, a lowly salesman, or even the humble office cleaner, you all have a routine. If there is a sudden, unexpected change, straight out of left-field and shattering the very structure of your life. How will you deal with it?

On the other hand, if you can only get up onto the Divine Mode you can see things differently. You can learn how to handle these unexpected shattering events in a calmer and more manageable manner.

I like to describe this **Default Mode** situation as living in the apartment we just described, reading this book and meditating, thinking things through. If perhaps a relative or a close friend comes along and says, 'Why are you living like this, in the middle of a jungle? It's much cheaper to live in the country. You can wake up with the birds singing, a river flowing with crystal clear water right outside your door, fresh air to breathe. You can open up your front door and go out into a meadow. What a wonderful feeling that would be, right? For the same price as an apartment in town, you can have a large house in the country. There, you can go to the top floor, look out at the wonderful scenery, maybe even a panoramic view'.

If you could do this, you would get that Wow! Sensation; fall in love with the world! And, more than likely, you would no longer be interested in the rat race. Wouldn't this be a wonderful way to live?

Perhaps, you would still get on the train and go into town to work. You would slip into the **Default Mode** and at the end of day, return to that new, fresh way of living. It could be a lot of effort and a lot of time spent travelling, but it would be worth it.

Many people change their lives; take up some new activity in order to earn a living much closer to their new home, their new lifestyle. It doesn't matter really when or what you do in this 'change' process, whether it be taking up art or agriculture, or setting up a factory way out in the countryside. When you do make a change, you have taken the first step towards changing your life.

Now, let us equate this and follow on with our imaginary town apartment scene. Walk outside of your new house, right now, instead of from your apartment in town. As you step into the sunshine outside, you suddenly realise that there are five stories above but no stairs to climb, and that staying downstairs kept you on the **Default Mode**.

Now in the countryside, with this change in your way of thinking, you divide your life between living on the ground floor in the **Default Mode**, as well as living on the first floor in the Divine Mode. It is not so simple though, because this house doesn't have any stairs either. However, there has been one fundamental change; you are now living in a different type of house, a home where we will be able to work together, building the stairs brick-by-brick, slowly moving up to the first floor and onto the Divine Mode.

The secret is to be able to stay there, on the first level, the Divine Mode. But, every now and again you have to change back to **Default Mode**. You just can't help it. There is a need for you to interact with other people, which is normal. You are never going to change so much so that you would be full time on the Divine Mode. It just doesn't work like that. And life doesn't allow you to do it. Would you really want to do that, always be in Divine Mode?

Whilst living downstairs on the **Default Mode**, but aspiring to move upstairs and onto the Divine Mode… together let's build those stairs to move up and change your life.

Look around you. Everything has changed. Suddenly you realise it is a beautiful world out there and you have given yourself more time to think.

Over my many years of research and travel, I have had a great number of experiences, taking me through hundreds of situations and more than a third of all the countries in the world.

I have been working in so many fields of activity I am able to talk your language almost whatever you do in life.

I have been there and done that

There are people in this world who work very hard, have no personal life to speak of and have traded much for success. Now you tell me, where does the success really lie? On the one hand the person who is ambitious, succeeds, but has no real life. When he comes to the end of his days what does he really have, what has he achieved? Sadly, soon after he retires or dies the rest of the world will forget about him and find a replacement.

You're probably thinking, 'Wait a minute! So what? I have plenty of time to achieve what I want to achieve. I even have time to make mistakes'. And you could be right, if you were living in the Divine Mode. You can live in the Divine Mode and you can have loads of time to make mistakes and make them right too. That is what we are in the process of teaching you - How to live on the Divine Mode.

But, most important of all, you must give yourself time to think. This is important in getting to the Divine Mode. You must stop, reflect, think, and wait for that special message. This is the most significant part, waiting for that message. There is a time to act and there is a time to step back. Always wait for the page to turn. It is important that you don't try to jump to conclusions and make important decisions as you conduct yourself in life on the **Default Mode**. Make your decisions on the Divine Mode.

Now, we're ready to meditate again, to go through what we have learned. After you have finished reading this chapter, close your eyes, lie back and think. Think about the alternatives available and choose whichever you prefer.

It is your choice. You can stay where you are, living with the four portals of the Soul, unreachable above you, and no stairs.

Or you can go to the countryside, as it were, with the realisation that this does not necessarily have to be a physical move. A lot depends on community, family and friends.

You would certainly make new friends once you enter the Divine Mode. Your family would always prefer to come and visit you in the countryside. It is for you to decide what you want in life.

That beautiful mansion in the countryside could be in a different country. Perhaps you have been dreaming of moving, living in South Africa, Australia or the United States. And from the United States you may want to move to England, from Singapore through to somewhere else. The options are limitless.

Each of us has our own perspective on life and that is great.

The people reading this book, perhaps in another language, live all across the globe. You would be surprised where they come from. It's quite incredible. Almost every country is represented.

So, everyone should ask this of themselves, 'Do I want to stay in my own country? Or change to another county, town or village. Maybe that will do the trick.

Never stay in a rut work on opening up your mind and expand to new horizons'.

This is what it's all about. You must have the determination not to be locked inside your spacesuit and the space that you are in.

Get out of that **Default Mode** and up onto the Divine Mode. Just sit down and think.

Perhaps after you have finished this meditation, take a piece of paper and a pen. Then write down, just for yourself, what type of life you would prefer to lead and where you would want to be. Use your imagination to see where you want to be in 6 months, a year, 5 years, even 25 years from now. Look forward and then get to your new life step-by-step.

This little exercise will help you a lot when moving to the next chapter, where I will take you even farther on this incredible journey.

Now get your Adrenaline running, draw down the energy from the Divine Just Stand-Up and Meditate

Now follow again the guide at the end of the previous chapter (see page 45).

Understand this basic lesson in life:

We all have a soul
deep down inside
Linked to the 'Divine Mode'
upwards we strive
Whilst attached to our spacesuit,
we are locked inside,
living in a world of chaos,
ego and strife
A slave to our body
for the rest of our life
Our souls have the power
to make the body its slave
Just keep in your mind
it's the Divine Mode we crave

Eliyahu Kelman

I can tap you on the side of your head
from the outside
But it is only you that can open up
from the inside.
I need to re-program your brain
to accept, absorb, internalise
the rules and secrets of life
Certainty Absolute Certainty
is the only way to go
Turning tables on the impossible
towards the Divine Mode you grow

Eliyahu Kelman

Chapter Four

Certainty, Absolute Certainty

- *Just arrived; no money, no job, no plan, no hope... All about creating your own opportunities*

- *Download the streaming messages; discover your inner abilities and act on them*

This is a very important rule, live it 24/7.

In all circumstances in life there is always a possibility of success. You only have to believe with Absolute Certainty. Believing this way will bring about a sure guarantee that you will succeed and overcome all your challenges, whatever they are. You need to Internalize this and make it part of your psyche.

This is the most basic lesson that we need to learn in order to get up to the Divine Mode.

Living on the Divine Mode and the getting up there is all about those repetitive habits.

As I have repeated again and again, for this journey towards your newly created design for living, while getting there you will feel the benefits of the Divine Mode. And each time you arrive, you will be very happy to remain on that higher level. When Osmosis eventually happens for you, you will know it, feel it and be in a Blissful-Space. We can then keep building even more stairs to help us get up to the next floor. This is what we need to work on, getting to this first stage and staying there, fully living on that level.

So what is the secret of **Certainty, Absolute Certainty**?

Unless and until we achieve this level of belief in ourselves, we simply will not be able to move forward.

Many people hesitate, doubting themselves, and their capabilities. Going into an exam, even before they have given themselves a chance to sit down to write, keep on repeating to themselves: 'Oh, I'm not going to succeed with this. I'm going to fail'.

I can guarantee one thing, right now, if you speak like that to yourself; you will most certainly fail.

But the person who really works hard and says to themselves, 'I'm going to pass this exam' or 'I'm going to get my degree' or 'I'm going to build a successful relationship with my future partner in life'. Continue to repeat this to yourself, 'I am going to succeed…' 'I am going to succeed…' - You will most certainly succeed.

> *Just keep repeating to yourself…*
> *'I will succeed, I will succeed'*
> *Internalize this,*
> *let it become a part of you,*
> *you will achieve*
> *a guaranteed level of success*

On the Divine Mode, whatever you want, providing it's right, you will achieve your goal. Nature and the Divine will join to help you to reach your goal, provided you are specific about what you want.

A story, I have told many times over, which shows how Absolute Certainty works, is one of a father who lived in Poland, an itinerant salesman, who would go from village to village selling his trinkets, making his living this way. One day, as he arrived at a new village, one that he had not visited before, he found himself in the middle of a celebration. It was the birthday of the local Duke, an aristocrat who owned the village, employed all the villagers and pretty much controlled their lives. The local people were in the midst of presenting the Duke with a donkey foal, a young donkey just weaned from its mother. The Duke knew that he couldn't, or actually wouldn't, take it home to his castle and so was in a dilemma as to how to deal with the foal.

Now our traveller selling his wares had two things he really wanted most in life: A donkey to ride on and carry his baggage, and just as important, a better life for his family. He hadn't thought much about how to get a donkey, but was presented with an opportunity that would help him in his life, but if '**Abra-Ca-Dabra**' was to work he needed to state clearly what he wanted.

The Duke saw the man, a stranger to the village, walking nearby, so called him over and instructed him to carry the donkey back to his castle. Now, the man saw an opportunity to offer his services to the Duke and the donkey as a possible reward, even if he would have to wait for the foal to grow up into a donkey, he would still get what he wanted. But in the bigger picture, he might get much more than that by associating himself with the Duke.

So, sometimes we want something, believing with Absolute Certainty that we will achieve it, though in the end the outcome isn't exactly as we had imagined. But we at times get something else, which usually turns out for the best.

Have you ever wondered how some people succeed in their studies, how others succeed in getting what they want from their life? We tell ourselves that it must be put down to intelligence or good luck.

There is no such thing as luck, good or bad. You make your success yourself, through help on the Divine Mode. Your good fortune is on the Divine Mode, where happenstance doesn't exist.

So what do you say now?

Are you still saying, 'He had good luck'. 'He came into an inheritance'. 'He had good connections or is smarter than me?'

None of that is true. If you really research into how people succeed in life, it is because they had **'Certainty, Absolute Certainly'**.

A General in the army may win a battle because he has Absolute Certainty, and not only because he has the chance of winning. Don't forget the General might still have a problem if the opposing army has a high level of certainty and training. If both Generals have high levels of certainty and command evenly matched professional armies, Divine intervention will play a much greater part.

You will see that most of the stories of **'Certainty, Absolute Certainty'** woven into this book are drawn from events from my own life. I have seen first-hand that success in life is rarely any of the other things that we talked about: intelligence, luck, connections, money, or even tricks.

It is one thing only: hard work requiring knowledge of the secrets we learn as we go through Chapter after Chapter and in addition, to understand what we are doing, because that is important too. Together with **'Certainly, Absolute Certainty'.** we will succeed.

We are now going to link **'Certainty, Absolute Certainty'** to freedom of choice. **Freedom of choice**[18], in this context, is when you choose which Certainty you want. In other words, there is no point in being certain if it is about something that you don't understand or something that you hadn't studied or researched, or is just simply not possible. You have the freedom of choice to decide what will be good for you, or at least what is achievable. That is another truth – an important secret and rule to live by.

> ***There is***
> ***nothing in life,***
> ***Absolutely Nothing,***
> ***that is out of reach***
> ***or cannot be achieved***
> ***just***
> ***Think… Stand-Up.. & Walk Tall***

In order to understand more clearly what it is like living on the **Default Mode**.

Just consider this story:

A peasant saw a beautiful princess and decided he wanted to marry her. It doesn't matter how certain he is and how much freedom of choice he has, he just doesn't have a chance to get anywhere near her.

So it is, when you are dealing with society, you must have the ambition and determination to get to the top, however this must be taken step-by-step. If you are an outsider, you have to first make yourself rich or famous and wait until you are accepted.

Let me put this into the right context. We are all given the same breath at the start of life; however some of us are born into families and societies that allow us to live a much more privileged life.

We all know that in the past things were different, to give an example: A non-European living in our world today has the same chance as someone born Caucasian would have. A few years back, people of Color were viewed as inferior to White people and had fewer opportunities. Today, we can see that whether you are Black or White, Indian, Chinese or essentially anybody who seems to be different, can have a lot of success by exploiting certainty, belief, hard work and perseverance.

Today the world has a different attitude to those who were viewed in a darker light. Even a person who comes from a very poor family, or is uneducated, has a chance to pull him or herself up to any level they desire.

So, life is not really all that restrictive. For women today, many have the freedom to climb to the top and many, many do.

But who climbs to the top? Is it the one who realises that they have a choice and acts accordingly, immersing themselves completely into their dream, hopefully not paying too high a price in their private and personal lives. Please remember we are not talking about 'winner takes all'. that is certainly not what living on the Divine Mode is all about. It is about living the life you want to live, without detriment to others and yourself.

Women can do a job, when applying Absolute Certainty anyone can do a job. In my experience, many times, I have seen women handle a task in a far superior fashion to their counterparts, men… I believe the main reason is as they apply their emotions and their unique sixth sense when Downloading Messages from the Big Brain.

There is a story that the Kabbalists tell, about a quiet man who lived in a small town. He had many followers who loved his traditions, stories and guidance. Loved by all, he wasn't by any means a man of great wealth. He would often rely on charity for survival; sometimes even chopping wood in the forest to earn some money. As was his family's tradition, Fridays and Saturdays were holy days and always spent with family. One day his wife came to him and told him that she had no food or money. She had Absolute Certainty that they would be granted a way to continue living on the level of tradition they had chosen for themselves.

He decided to visit his friend, a particularly wealthy man. He tapped on his window and when no one came to the door, he quietly walked away. The friend, who had been busy inside, eventually came to the door and saw his friend walking away. He ran after him and stopped him with a gentle touch to the shoulder.

'Where are you going? Why didn't you wait a while for me to come to the door?'

The simple man explained his predicament and again the wealthy friend asked why he didn't wait a little longer for him.

'I knew with Absolute Certainty that I would be helped. It didn't matter whether I waited by your window or walked away'.

He laughed and gave money to go buy food for his family.

The point of the story is to reiterate that you cannot just wait around for something to happen. You have to take a step, just as the poor man did. He took a step towards finding a solution and with certainty he found one.

The only way to survive
and overcome challenges
Believe in your destiny,
freedom of choice
Think of the possibilities,
putting negativity aside
Move forward with certainty,
just go for the ride
Play your life through,
it's like a game of chess,
a magic solution,
bringing on success

Eliyahu Kelman

Freedom of Choice [18]
and
Certainty, Absolute Certainty

Let me relate a personal story where Absolute Certainty took centre stage:

I had returned to London from Singapore, where I had been Principal of a school, at that time very prestigious but not well paid. I had a very good job lined up as a director of a major insurance and trust company. My immediate problem was that I had no money, a young family to support and a three-month gap to fill before my new job started.

So, what did I do?

I still had my visiting card as Principal of the school, so I went to the West End in London to look around while trying to figure out what to do; I was waiting while expecting messages to download showing me how to overcome this challenge.

I found myself standing outside a branch of Avis Rent-a-Car and had a feeling that I should go inside. I did, even though I had absolutely no idea what I was planning to do once inside. I found a secretary and said, 'I want to see your Manager, please give him this business card'. The card worked and in no time I was sitting in front of the man in charge.

I found myself telling him that I hadn't come to rent a car, as I didn't have the cash for that. I told him that I had a job, but that it wouldn't start for three months and I needed to earn some money in the meantime. I then said that I spoke quite a number of languages and asked if they needed somebody who could meet cruise ships as they arrived in port, set up a pop-up office and rent out cars to passengers on the cruise ships. I was absolutely certain that I was not going to walk out of there empty handed, even though they hadn't advertised any such job.

He looked me straight in the eye and said, 'How did you know that I was trying to figure out how I could get somebody to do exactly that?'

Within a few hours I had been given a car and was driving to meet a cruise ship due in that evening on the other side of the country. For those three months I worked very hard and earned a good deal of money. I was a young man then and often travelled overnight between ships and every time I drove, the more mileage I did, the more money I made (not to mention the tips!).

From adventure to adventure,
throughout my life,
ignoring realities,
chaos and strife

Always remember,
we are not what we do,
we always retain our special hue

With hidden personalities inside,
always creating opportunities,
for success we must strive
Overcoming obstacles
The only way to survive

Eliyahu Kelman

Up
on the
Divine Mode
you are never alone
Always have your radar up,
be ready to download messages [19]
never let your ego get in the way
There is always something
waiting to happen

Eliyahu Kelman

Whenever you find yourself in a hole there is no reason to sit back and do nothing. You have to have Absolute Certainty in whatever you do, be positive, and if you take that step forward, you will always be helped.

If you don't take that step, but just sit back and wait, thinking, 'Well, I don't have a job or an income and I don't know what to do, so I will just wait and see what happens'.

With that approach you won't get anything done and the problem, or rather challenge won't go away.

Certainty is what I had when I walked in to Avis that day, and I knew I was starting to download a streaming message.

Too many people go into freeze mode, shocked at the situation they are in, not knowing how to move forward, so they just stay where they are. When I gave my business card to the secretary I had no idea what I was going to say, but while I waited to see the Manager, I received a direct download from the Big Brain. As I spoke to him I was hearing my words for very first time. It was my Absolute Certainty that kept me talking and allowed the idea to stream into my head. A constant downloading of words that I used to form the idea.

When I learnt to combine: Certainty, together with Downloading Messages and not allowing my ego to get in the way, I was helped to continue making a respectable living for my family.

Think about that very carefully.

Now we are ready for our end of chapter Self-Meditation. But, this time, we require a different type of meditation.

What I want you to do, is to take the same position as last time, sit comfortably, ensure you have no restrictions or interruptions, loosen your tie, undo your shirt collar, take off your shoes and relax.

And where do we go in order to relax? We go up above time, space and motion. We go up above all the challenges we have here in the **Default Mode** and in this so-called reality. Now, start to think about the different problems you have to solve. Remember what I taught you. You never call them problems. They are challenges.

> *Remove the word 'PROBLEMS'*
> *from your vocabulary*
> *As of today you are*
> *dealing with challenges*
> *Carefully select those challenges*
> *worth fighting for*

Think about them one by one and you can be certain that there is a solution sitting out there, just waiting to be discovered. You may not know it now, but if you think carefully and go through those challenges one by one, you will realise there is no reason to sit still and do nothing about them.

> *You will be helped to move*
> *forward in the direction*
> *you have decided to go*

You will receive a lot of support on the Divine Mode. All you have to do, right now, is just concentrate, focus and believe.

Even if you haven't made up your mind as to which way you are going, turn it over in your mind a few times. It is for you to map out your own destiny and the solutions will be downloaded.

One of my favourite poems really sums it all up. There are a number of versions recorded on Google.

This is mine adapted to fit, I will never forget it and I hope you won't either.

Upon the plains of opportunity,
whiten the bones of countless thousands
Who,
whilst on the threshold of success,
hesitated, waited,
and while waiting sat down and died

Once the Soul awakens,
begin the search and never go back
Soar upwards towards new heights,
on the Divine Mode
Leave behind a life of
complacency, chaos
and ego of the Default Mode
You will never again be held back
by any danger or challenge,
whilst striving towards
the summit of fulfilment

Eliyahu Kelman

Chapter Five

ABRA-Ca-DABRA

Three Powerful Words from ancient Aramaic - 'I create as I speak' - Properly harnessed they can affect your life and that of all those around you

- *A little known secret, enabling control over any outcome - positive or negative*

- *How to take control, overcome conflict and avoid hidden stumbling blocks*

- *An awareness of what really controls our lives and the world we live in*

I want to share another secret with you and I am sure that you will be more than surprised to read this. Many people are simply not aware of the other aspect of **Certainty, Absolute Certainty**, and that it is linked to the word **Abra-Ca-Dabra**.

Abra-Ca-Dabra, what has it got to do with this subject? It is a well-known fact that **Abra-Ca-Dabra** has been used generation after generation in so-called magical presentations.

They take a wand and declare in a dramatic voice. '**Abra-Ca-Dabra**' and magically a rabbit will appear in a hat or someone will disappear. We all know that it is trickery; a slight of the hand or misdirection but, every child and adult alike, loves the entertainment.

No one seems to be aware of the fact that **Abra-Ca-Dabra** happens to be Aramaic.

No challenge exists without a solution
Streaming messages downloaded
full of intention
Choosing the soul to develop
its hidden potential,
for brilliant ideas and
a life of invention
Mankind is not the inventor,
nor the source of it all
Ideas and solutions are
not ours to recall
It's Abra-Ca-Dabra hidden inside
Dream and imagine…
Go with the tide

Eliyahu Kelman

We have already discussed the fact the 'speech is all powerful' and must be taken seriously. It is so powerful that we are able to influence the outcome by what we say.

Abra-Ca-Dabra does not grant unlimited power to just anyone. It must come together with Absolute Certainty when we are using this tool in our own lives. We must be careful what we say, because what is uttered from our lips takes on a power of its own. To withdraw or take back is almost impossible and is Kabbalah on a much higher level.

> *You are master of your words*
> *before you speak*
> *The whole world becomes its master*
> *once you have spoken,*
> *be careful what you say*
> *You might unleash the enormous power*
> *of Abra-Ca-Dabra*
> *Bringing into reality*
> *what you say – What you speak*

The story of the Titanic is well known and there are many films and books published on the subject, the psychological background version as well as the real life historic tale. Recreating the events and life on board as the ship sunk was based on the interviews with the few survivors and a psychological understanding of what must have gone on during those last dramatic moments.

Did you know that the Titanic was supposed to be a ship that was unsinkable? In its day it was the most modern ship in the world. At a specially arranged dinner party the night before the launch of this 'unsinkable ship'. the captain stood to give the keynote speech. Many influential people were there; the press, dignitaries, shareholders, people with money and people involved in building the ship. The pre-launch party was attended by a few thousand people.

The captain stood up and said, 'This ship is so safe that even G-d cannot sink it'.

Bang!
The die was cast!
His words were spoken
Abra-Ca-Dabra
He sealed the fate of the ship.

You do not challenge the Master of the world. The **Divine** created the Seas; The icebergs; all of the knowledge and inspiration of the designers and engineers; all of the raw materials together with the surrounding skills that made the Titanic possible.

Arrogance, pride and ego made them forget that all their success is derived from creation.

You do not challenge the Divine.

I have no idea why they celebrated before going on a maiden voyage.

They celebrated - It sunk.

It would have made more sense for them to celebrate after they had arrived at their destination.

I believe that there was much arrogance in the air that evening, from the captain, the engineers, the shipping company and the investors too. They all trumpeted the superb engineering and the effort that had been put into making it the unsinkable liner. I have no doubt that it was a beautiful ship and I take my hat off to all involved in engineering such a magnificent display of human intelligence. But one cannot mess with nature and the Divine. One cannot, even with the best materials available in this world, nor all the money that was spent on building the ship and even with the considerable sums of money that the passengers would have spent. One cannot challenge the Divine. Just with one statement of an **Abra-Ca-Dabra**, the captain jinxed the liner and all the lives of the passengers and staff.

Remember, 'I will create as I speak' and when it is a challenge blurted out like that the outcome was inevitable.

I am not saying that this was a punishment. That would be the last thing I would want to suggest to you, but it shows you how careful you have to be with your words.

Many Kabbalists and Sages actually have the insight and capability to influence the outcome of events - over life and death, success or failure. Whether interpreting a dream, giving advice, warning that someone will become ill or die within a certain period, survive adversity, or live long and prosper; that's exactly what would happen.

Pay attention to what they have to say...

On their level messages are pervasive, streaming into their minds... into their dreams...

Sages and Kabbalists, having
profound knowledge
and understanding of
the hidden secrets and rules
of the universe,
as revealed and laid down
in ancient writings,
together with the embedded nature
of Abra-Ca-Dabra
– I create as I speak –
Have reached a level that makes
the outcome
of their words inevitable

We can take a lesson from this
There is a big difference between
wisdom and understanding
Most people have wisdom
in one form or another
Understanding is something
you cannot possess
Without your Soul functioning
on the Divine Mode
with open channels
to the Big Brain

Eliyahu Kelman

I have another little story, coming from the Aggadah texts, about an older and a younger man standing together on the seashore, watching the crowds waving off a ship as it departed on its maiden voyage. Everyone was making a big fuss without really knowing what was going to happen on the voyage, and if indeed its outcome would be successful. At the same time another passenger ship arrived from a distant port, tying up at its mooring without any fuss or welcoming ceremony. The older man remarked that this was strange and that it should have been the other way round.

It would have been better to celebrate the end of a successful journey, than throw a party as the ship departed on its voyage into the unknown. Celebrations should have been left until after the ship's successful arrival at its final destination.

It is the same thing with life and death. When a person dies his or her life should be celebrated. Whilst welcoming a baby into the world without really knowing how he or she will turn out and match up to all of life's challenges, achievements, health, wealth, family; which King will win the fight for control of this new human being just born? Will the journey through life end up on the Divine Mode or down below on the **Default Mode**?

Winston Churchill was a master of the English language. We will always remember him for his famous speeches of encouragement and positive predictions. His words moved people. His words saved England from destruction. His words gave courage to people who felt they had no opportunities in life. His words helped many believe that they could survive the blitz and the attack from Germany.

Churchill's famous speeches in Parliament moved the people. They were both sharp and intelligent. If there is any example in this world of somebody using the power of **Abra-Ca-Dabra**, it was Churchill, but he always used it for the good. When he said that Hitler was going to war, only the Americans believed him.

The rule:

Be careful of what you say,
before you make use of
the power of Abra-Ca-Dabra

Now, before I digress too much, let me remind you of what we have to do and what we have to say.

'I am on the Divine Mode. Whatever I say will be created'.

But don't forget one thing.

Evil people must be believed too. There are bad people out there who believe with Absolute Certainty, and make use of **Abra-Ca-Dabra**. They can afflict terrible damage onto others and the world around them. If you are living in times of war or poverty, then what is said can work either against you or for you, but at the end of the day, it is up to you to control what you say and believe.

You have to listen to what people are saying, but listen especially to what you are saying, because **Abra-Ca-Dabra** is extremely powerful.

Whenever you combine **Abra-Ca-Dabra** with **Certainty, Absolute Certainty**, the combination of the two will certainly have you gaining control of your life. Things will change according to what you say with absolute certainty. Your life will change, so long as the **Abra-Ca-Dabra** is only used for the good, excluding everything else.

I had many friends who survived the Nazi concentration camps. Many people died and many survived, and here I am not thinking only about Jewish people. Whenever I spoke with a survivor, I would ask, 'How is it that you survived and others didn't?' In my mind, it wasn't only Eichmann saying, 'Left or right? This one lives and that one dies'.

Everybody received the same terrible food. Everybody was treated in the same way, whether going through winter without heating and only the thinnest of clothing or going through a stifling summer without any means to cool down. Why did some live and others die?

What I discovered was interesting. The difference was that those who died had given up. They were convinced that the Nazis would rule the world.

Their wives, families and children had been destroyed, their businesses gone and their jobs lost. They felt that they had nothing to live for. They had no hope, they couldn't see the war ever ending, and if it ever did, it would end badly.

People could not possibly survive with attitudes like that. They eventually died of depression and essentially, committed suicide.

But, what about those who survived? All of them, every last one had total and complete certainty that there was good in the world and that eventually all would be well, and that the war would end and in a good way. They had positive thinking. Those that survived believed that they would make it.

We can ask, 'Why does this happen? Why does this evil side of the world always strive to take over the good in this world?' It is the prevailing battle between the Sons of Light and the Sons of Darkness, an entirely different subject, and for another time.

Those people who survived had certainty that it would end, certainty that good would come out of it, certainty that they could still contribute to society and so they fought. Some were very ill and couldn't really ever get better, but many succeeded in later life. They knew they had to fight. They knew that everything could be taken away from them as it had in past. They knew that they had to protect their families because they too could be removed from their lives – just like that!

Coupled with this, I must mention that in life, tragedy can strike at any time, just like it did during that war, just like it did in the Vietnam war or even simpler, but no less tragic, when someone falls ill or dies following an accident.

How many millions of people, over the world, have petty fights over all sorts of little stupid things? How many people speak a harsh word, only to regret it later? And how many of those concentration camp survivors truly regretted having behaved badly towards other people. Little aware that those same people would be transported to the gas chambers, or into sheer slavery before they had a chance to put things right.

The important message in all of this is:

> **Think before you speak,**
> **think before you react,**
> **always take the time,**
> **to talk things over...**
> **Find a way to understand,**
> **if not to forgive**

Eliyahu Kelman

Always ask yourself, 'What would I do if that person, who I feel such hatred for, or with whom I am so angry and have decided to completely cut off any relationship with, were to suddenly be in a car accident left badly injured and could possibly die?

You may run over to them and try to apologise before it is too late. But, if you had just thought it through carefully before you reacted, you wouldn't have to be in that position.

And so, I urge you to have awareness all the time, of what you say and of what you do and more importantly, of what you think. That awareness is extremely important.

Meditation time.

And now we have to reflect and Internalize on these powerful thoughts and wonderful stories.

If we carry on doing this, by the end of our voyage together, every one of us would have changed and gained in some form or another. Then and only then will you start to see the true effect of the power of your thoughts and actions.

So, please, sit back, relax, get yourself comfortable, make sure you lock the door and cut out any sounds that would disturb you and let us go up to our special place. Let us go back out into space and let's meditate on the important things that we have learnt. When we are up in space, we can see the beautiful tapestry that was created of the world. We can afford to forget about the knots and tangles of the chaos below us.

We have left all of that behind; this gives us the possibility to free ourselves of those things that are pulling us down. We can just concentrate on the good and wonderful things in our lives. Even more important we can also do something about changing our life.

To get up onto the Divine Mode, to build more steps and floors, requires that we think about all that we have read here today, all the stories and all the beautiful messages.

We have to reflect very carefully on Certainty, the Absolute Certainty. Think of the occasions in your life and think of those times in other people's lives, when **Abra-Ca-Dabra** was effective. Think of **Abra-Ca-Dabra** in real life. This great idea of **Abra-Ca-Dabra** gets me quite excited, as it is so unique.

Just remember and analyse what you said today that you didn't have to say, and what you didn't say but should have said. Concentrate on that. You have to do an accounting summary of your life. Do not allow yourself to be overdrawn even overnight.

Just Stand-Up and Meditate

Concentrate on the picture on the cover of this book, which is a quiet peaceful forest out in the countryside. You can feel, hear, and almost touch the silence. Now **Stand-Up**, close your eyes, and imagine that you are one of the trees out there in our very private forest.

Now start swaying slowly back and forth, just like a tree in the wind. Pull your head back and push your mind higher and higher. Hold this position for a few minutes. With concentration, you will actually start to feel the force of your Soul and mind standing 'taller and taller'.

In the beginning, you will find it difficult to hold the 'upward' movement and will feel your mind slipping down. Keep focusing on the space high up above your head and concentrate on just pushing up.

Sway back and forth, back and forth ever so slowly like a tree in the wind. This will help you to connect with your Soul. Now start drawing down energy from the Divine Mode. Open your hands, palms upwards, stretching out from the sides of your body. Receive the energy forces generated from the Divine.

Concentrate on receiving the energy , feel your hands starting to get warmer. Concentrating on the upward movement, the swaying, and receive the downloaded energy into the palms of your hands; **repeat this exercise.**

Just remember the hidden message in that old street urchin's ditty:
'Sticks and stones may break my bones but words will never hurt me'

The truth is:

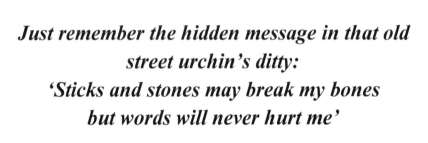

Sticks and stones may break my bones,
but words can definitely hurt me
If it hurts you,
it hurts other people as well

Each one of us possess
a hidden power beyond belief,
an unlimited capacity
We can make almost anything happen
Search deep into our inner self,
find out who we really are

Imagine the possibilities, turn them into realities
Unleash the secrets to re-program our minds,
eliminate all brain pollution,
focus on what we really want do with our lives

Eat it, drink it, sleep it, dream it
ever keeping this vision in our minds

Abra Ca Dabra
A power to be used for the good

Whatever we think and say with
Certainty, Absolute Certainty
will just like magic, morph
into a wonderful reality

Eliyahu Kelman

'I
believe
that the
greatest truths
of the universe
don't lie outside,
in the 'study of
stars and planets'.
They lie deep within us,
in the magnificence of
our Heart, Mind and Soul.
Until we understand what is within,
we can't understand what is without'.

Anita Moorjani

Chapter Six

The Incredible Story of Paul:

- *From modern-day Highwayman to Successful Businessman*

Throughout my life I have come across some fantastic people. I often think about Paul and his amazing story, not many of us get to meet really interesting and enigmatic people, like Paul.

At the time I was the International General Agent for a Fortune 100 public company, working from their corporate office in New York.

One day, Paul turned up at the office, a giant of a man. He was as tall as was wide. His skin coloring was dark; I found out later that he had both an Indian and a Jewish heritage. The one outstanding aspect about Paul was that, while he was huge man, often related to being rough and tough, Paul was a real gentle giant. He was a lovely young man with a big smile and a warm personality to boot. He was, perhaps, one of the gentlest people I have ever met in my life. I fell in love with his crazy character and all that came with it.

He told me that he was an inventor and had had a number of brilliant ideas, some of these he wanted to show and share with me. We got on so well that he invited my wife and I to his estate in Michigan.

Besides finding myself intrigued with Paul and his life, I could only imagine what a fruitful tale it will turn out to be; I was also sussing him out for business purposes. I had learned, through past experiences, that if you want to consult for a company, you have to spend time trying to understand more about who wants to consult with you and what makes them tick. Learning how and why they think the way they do is key to a successful business relationship. There is no other way one can achieve success.

One has to be very certain about everyone you are dealing with. There is always a reason to check and to see if there is any message download of either a warning or a 'thumbs up'. Experiencing feelings is very important. I mentioned, in an earlier chapter, the bankers smell test, this can be equated to a gut feeling or when you are attuned to the Divine Mode, that downloadable message.

There is an Old Russian saying that Ronald Reagan loved to use, 'Trust, but verify'. This is the most effective way that any relationship can be established.

Paul had a beautiful, impressive house on his vast estate and his own yacht. We had such a wonderful time together, especially the first night when we sat down and he told me his story, and what a story it was. I still get a very particular feeling when I think back and remember.

In addition to being the Pastor of a small country church, Paul had built a very impressive factory near his estate, where he employed several hundred people. As his process was unique, he had even designed the specialised core equipment himself. He had already expanded internationally, building a factory in India, which at that time employed more than a thousand workers.

As the story developed, it became clear that Paul was already up on the Divine Level and was downloading his own streaming messages continuously. As an evangelical Pastor, his every word was infused with spirituality. He was a most captivating person to listen to.

His story unfolded as we talked through the night. I am not going to take all night to tell you this amazing story. I will give you the shorter version…

Picture Paul as a teenager, his father and mother had died at a young age, and he was left to fend for himself, foraging on the streets of America. When he had no choice, he would steal, but just enough to survive. He would make sure he had a place to sleep and food to eat.

But survive he did.

I was shocked to hear that over two million people live like this, on the streets of the United States, the last place on earth where one would expect to find this.

At that time Paul had acquired a horse and a gun. Strangely enough, in that modern age, he became a Highwayman, a Road Agent. He was, to all intents and purposes, an old-style bandit who stole from travellers. He would hold people up, especially if they were driving on a lonely country road. He would walk away with whatever he could, usually food and a little bit of money, but he never actually hurt anybody. There were times, though, when he would cry because he knew he frightened people. But Paul was a survivor and his mission was to survive in any manner that he could. That was how he justified himself.

But to me, Paul never tried to justify his actions.

Sure, his sermons would often feature his own personal experiences, used as wake-up calls to all those Americans who were indifferent to the plight of the dispossessed.

I have often heard it remarked that these people chose this way of life, while knowing full well that a lot of them were victims of society that condoned profitable stripping by Banks and lawyers in foreclosures endorsed by the legal system. Unfortunately the good and decent members of the legal profession are unfairly damaged by this reputation

But let us see how the story develops.

One freezing night during the cold winter months, a time when not many would dare venture outside. Most sensible people would be at home, huddled around their home fires and not out on the cold, dangerous roads. This was, of course, not good for Paul, who then couldn't rob anyone. One winter's night he and his horse were meandering around, tired, hungry and cold, searching for food and shelter. Very late that night, he reached a small church perched on a hill, with only a little house for company, which he assumed was occupied by the local Pastor and his family.

Knocking on the door, his prayers were answered when the Pastor opened it.

The Pastor spoke first,

'What can I do for you, my son?''

Standing there, shivering in the cold, Paul asked for food and a place to sleep.

The Pastor invited him in, whilst his daughter served him a simple hot meal the Pastor dug out some dry clothes for Paul, to exchange for his old and soaking wet clothing. They were really very kind to him, choosing to ignore his gun whilst they fed him and found a place in the stable for his very bedraggled horse.

Just imagine. Would you feel safe taking in a complete stranger?

Knowing he had a gun?

Seeing he had a horse

Would you feel safe?

Would you accept a stranger into your house, to eat and sleep there and still feel safe?

The old Pastor believed that G-d would only send him opportunities to help other people, and that no harm would come to him or his family.

The Pastor and his daughter spoke to Paul about their lives and Paul opened up and told them everything about himself, his parents, his struggle to survive, and the inevitability of the descent into his current way of life. While he was doing this, he found himself falling in love, for the first time in his life, with the Pastor's daughter…

As Paul tossed and turned all that night, he wondered how on earth he could possibly win her over and at the same time persuade the Pastor to be his father-in-law… Paul didn't believe he had a chance.

The next day he was back on his horse and on his way, feeling much fresher and well rested (and invigorated by love). As he continued with his way of life he couldn't get the girl out of his mind.

Thinking the way he did, and believing that he had little chance of getting the Pastor to agree, he felt he had no choice but to kidnap the daughter; after all that is what Highwaymen do.

After several sleepless nights he saddled up and rode back to the little church on the hill, where he planned to capture her early in the morning, just as she would go out to draw water from the well in the churchyard. In the meantime he broke into the church, intending to go ahead with his plan.

As he climbed in through a window and stepped to the floor of the church, he was almost blinded by a light shining onto a large mass of people, tens of thousands, all dressed in white and kneeling in prayer. Overwhelmed by his vision, knowing full well that the people couldn't possibly be in that tiny church for real, he got down on his knees and cried. He was so affected by the intensity of the vision and shining light ahead that he cried himself to sleep on the floor of the church.

In his dreams, he heard the voice of his father for the first time since he was a small boy.

'You know, Paul, your mother and I loved you. It was unfortunate that we died early. We didn't want that to happen, but we had no control, believe me. But, up here it is wonderful just living as a Soul. We are no longer suffering and that is a beautiful feeling. Paul, we love you. You just received a message that you have to change, but you have to have certainty that you can change. You have to build up your life and you'll get Divine inspiration. You will get messages, which you have to follow. The most important message you already have - Marry that girl! This is your destination in life'

The dream of his father vanished and he woke up.

He realised as he woke up that he had overslept and the Pastor's daughter had come in to clean the church and prepare for the morning prayers. To her great surprise she saw Paul there in the locked church.

'Paul, what are you doing here?'

He told her the truth.

'I couldn't get you out of my mind. I am in love with you! You have no reason to be in love with me, but I am in love with you, and I came back to kidnap you. I want to ride off into the sunset with you and never return. I wanted to tell your father, but I didn't know how to talk to him and what to say, so I decided this was the next best plan'.

She was so overwhelmed with emotion and as it was, after all, very romantic. He was like a prince, although not exactly dressed like a prince, but he was a prince nevertheless, with a horse, who wanted to kidnap and marry her.

He urged her to sit with him and told her all about his dream. He told her all about his life, the good things and the bad things. He told her about the vision and the words of his father in his dream.

'I promise you, if you marry me, I will change and leave my current life. I will just forget all about it'.

As you can imagine, she was very, very touched. Here was a simple country girl with romantic dreams, whose knight on a white charger had just arrived! She just could not resist, so fell in love with Paul as well.

Paul was still concerned about how her father would respond and so he asked her, 'How are we going to tell your father?'

She continued… 'You were frank with me and you won me over. Don't worry. My father is a good man. We are going to tell him exactly what happened and you will see that he will react well'.

Together they walked from the church to the house, just as the Pastor was opening the door. Not knowing what had gone on before, he welcomed him back, offering him a good hearty breakfast.

'Well Paul, what are you doing here?' The gentle Pastor asked whilst they were eating.

Together, his daughter and Paul told him the whole story. And the Pastor reacted exactly as his daughter had predicted.

'Listen, my son, I'd better train you to be my assistant. You speak very well and you could help me to run the church. Somehow or other, we will manage on the meagre income that we have to live on'.

He was, of course, thinking what would be best for his daughter.

As we know, it is so easy if you are born into a good family. It is so easy if your way of life is on the Divine from the moment you are born.

But, somebody who changes their life, somebody who decides to go from the **Default Mode** to the Divine Mode, must be very special.

Because he had been there, done that, and then left evil for good.

The Pastor, respecting Paul for his honesty, said: 'You will influence many people with your story. That is why I am willing to share the little we have with you', and he welcomed him in.

They had a very small congregation, only about 50 families, after all they were way out in the country, a very rural area, they all came together to celebrate the marriage of Paul and the Pastor's daughter. The realities of their lifestyle didn't allow them the luxury of just living happily ever after. Paul worked very hard in the church, trying to make a living. He soon realised that he needed to find additional ways to support the family. So, he went out to rummage the garbage dumps, an activity he was very used to during his previous life. He sorted through the rubbish to see if he could find something interesting, something that he could use or sell.

Every day, he used his father-in-law's truck and went out to look with the hope of picking up something interesting. One day, he came across an old refrigeration room. He was convinced that he would be able to convert it into an oven, by running the refrigeration process in reverse. He organised a group from the congregation to bring his find back to the house by the church.

An idea started to stream into his mind. If he could convert this into an oven he would be able to create something new and original using it. Paul, with his insightful mind, started putting a plan together, which involved plastic, all the plastic he had been picking up from the dumps. His idea was to make mirrors out of plastic.

Little did he know, then, that this would be the first time in history that someone would succeed in combining a patented substance with plastic, in such a way as to successfully create flexible mirrors.

With his vision of the little church filled with thousands of lights still in his mind, he was motivated by the desire to line the walls of the church with mirrors, so creating the effect he desired.

And that is how it all started. He continued to work hard, carried on scouring the dumps, finding things to sell. Eventually he made a breakthrough with the plastic mirrors. He succeeded in setting up the mirrors in the church, which created the illusion that the church was much bigger than it actually was.

One of the members of the congregation came to him and said, 'You know, Paul, we all love you because you are so determined. We all know where you came from and we think we know where you are going. You have succeeded with this so I am going to fund you to set up a small workshop to produce mirrors. You can work at night making mirrors and during the day you can go out to sell them'.

The man continued, 'But I have one condition. You must register a patent. I will give you the money to do this, because if anybody catches on to what you're doing, without that registered patent, they can take away everything you worked so hard for. It could be very valuable one day, so I want you to get a patent'.

The next morning Paul went to the local patent office and found the Assistant to the Registrar, who was buried in paperwork.

The young man felt Paul's presence. Looking up he saw a giant of a man looming over him with an enormous smile on his face; the conversation went like this.

'I came in to register a patent'.

'Why don't you sit down, Sir. You know, you look like someone that I would like to help. Now what did you invent? Show me the drawings'.

'I have no drawings'. Paul said.

'Then show me the formula'.

'I don't have a formula, but I know how to make it'.

'Well, what do you make?'

Paul explained to the man what it was that he had made…

'You can't register that!'

'I can't register it? What do you mean I can't register it?'

'You can't register that because scientifically it is impossible!'

Paul laughed and told the man, 'Well, thank G-d I didn't know it was impossible when I started out, because then I would never have tried'.

The enthusiastic young man was dumbfounded. 'Really! You are actually making them already? Well, whatever you say it is still impossible. Let me come and see how you make these mirrors. I have a strong feeling that you could have something there. I will help you to make up the drawings and will submit the applications for you. That is if this is really real'.

So the man went to see Paul's workshop, still a sceptic, but prepared to give Paul a chance. To his very great surprise he saw that Paul knew how to make mirrors, and beautiful mirrors at that, in all different shapes and colours of plastic, so he helped him to register the patent.

Well, the Patent Registrar had an enormous job to get it done. He kept on getting feedback from higher management at the Patent Office along the lines of, '…it's impossible'. Even after sending samples, he had to invite his superiors to come and take a look at the workshop, as he had done. Eventually they got the patent registered.

Paul's business rapidly grew, leading up to Paul moving his workshop from the back of the church to the current plant, where I spent a number of days discussing future strategies with Paul.

Now, all over the world, you will see Paul's mirrors in hotels and public places. The reason plastic mirrors are preferred over glass mirrors…, because they are less prone to dangerous breakage. A plastic mirror will not shatter and can be produced in an almost infinite number of shapes.

Now, why did Paul want to see me in the first place? Why was he interested in getting my support? He had money in the Bank. He was in a good financial position. He was happy, living in a beautiful part of the country and on the Divine Mode.

You know why he wanted to me to come and spend so much time with him? He had two new inventions that targeted different markets and needed strategic partners to make them work.

The first was a mirror, which enabled people to see around corners. This was a 180-degree mirror, if you think carefully you will know that you have seen these mirrors all over the world, in supermarkets, warehouses, maybe at the side of a country lane, wherever they can contribute to safety by warning the oncoming vehicle that another is coming towards them around the bend – many use Paul's invention.

This he had already developed, so I advised him that he didn't need any help from us. I told him to find an International Distributor and not to give away his core business. This was a gift from the Divine, for him and nobody else.

The second invention was an extremely efficient mirror to concentrate solar energy more effectively. It would be useful in generating electricity or heating water. This invention needed a substantial investment just to scratch the surface of the opportunity, he needed strategic partners who specialised in these fields; and this was what our company did for a living.

What is the secret behind this fantastic story?

First of all, Paul carried on running the church. His father-in-law eventually died and Paul had his own family and children to support.

Paul told me this after he had finished with his magical story.

'I changed my life because of what happened here at the church. I won the wife I wanted because it all happened here at the church. The Highwayman is part of my dim, distant past. I have certainly combined living on the Divine Mode with the **Default Mode**, as you have so clearly explained. I have a business and I am running a factory on the **Default Mode**, but I make sure that I always remember the source of my inspiration and my success'.

What are the two central themes to this story?

One is all the way **Certainty, Absolute Certainty**, **Abra-Ca-Dabra** in its highest form. Just remember what he said to the Patent Attorney when he was told that his invention was scientifically impossible.

'Had I known it was scientifically impossible, I wouldn't have done it. I wouldn't have even tried. Thank G-d I didn't know'.

Certainty, Absolute Certainty has always been the central theme of Paul's life. You can see it every step of the way.

As a Highwayman, even though a less than honourable profession, he was certain he would not be caught; even for this you need Divine protection. Even if nobody shoots at you but if you are picked up, your life would be ruined completely.

He married, built a family, and became a Pastor, an inventor, a businessman, all of this with **Certainty, Absolute Certainty**, combined with **Abra-Ca-Dabra**. As he spoke he created. Paul was very much aware of his right to freedom of choice, and faced with the reality presented in his vision and dream he chose to live on the Divine Mode.

From that day in the church, after the vision, for every step in his life he only chose the good and to live on the Divine Mode. That is an important message to meditate on and to think about.

We must meditate and perform Self-Hypnosis on ourselves. We have to repeat that meditation as many times as possible. Without meditation, the stories will remain memorable, but won't change your life.

So, it is necessary to think and internalize.

Drive the meditation forward until you experience the osmosis effect.

Now, we're going to meditate on everything we learnt from Paul's story, and on how it relates to our lives.

Find a comfortable chair and start to relax. Make sure that there will be no disturbances, lock the door, sit down, relax and picture where you are right now, and where you want to be.

It is so easy. You have done this several times before. You know what to expect, the stars, the planets and all that beauty, a silence that you can actually hear.

When you are ready we will transport ourselves up to a much higher level. It is a tough world out there, but up here on the Soul level, we have left that all behind. This is the place we all have to escape to, lying deep within our minds, our inner space.

Concentrate on creating this image and feeling right inside your head. By doing so, you have sent your Soul up to the Divine Mode. Concentrate on attaining a feeling that the real you, your Soul, is actually separated from your body.

Picture your life as it is today. Think of the changes you could make, what would you really like to do and what would you like to achieve? Just think of Paul and his life. Be convinced, even the Impossible is Possible.

Carry on visualising the picture you want to paint, think of every aspect of the life you would really like to lead. Make a plan in your mind, and be certain that you can and will be the main player in this picture.

Just remember that it is you that must plan your own voyage in life, knowing full well that when you reach a destination it is only a stepping-stone to the next one. There will be changes and you will have other ideas, but at the moment try to think of what you want to do now.

An important rule, embedded within the instructions given by G-d to Abraham.

'Get up early in the morning, and go to the place that I will show you...' (Genesis 22, 2).

In other words you must make the first move, do it with certainty, start moving forward and you will download messages from the Big Brain showing you the direction you should go, and what must be done on the way on the Divine Mode.

Think…
Stand-Up..
& Walk Tall
into your future
starting on your journey
with Certainty, Absolute Certainty
Streaming messages
instructing you which way to go
and what you must do

Nobody, but nobody, can decide for you what is in your best interests.

Lean on yourself, not others, because at the end of the day you are the only one who is going to have to live with yourself for the rest of your life. Never say anything is beyond your reach. Whatever you really want, you must have certainty that you are going to get it.

With determination and living on the Divine Mode, suddenly things start to happen. Just look at the story of Paul, cold, hungry, forlorn, lonely and without a past, present or future. Suddenly life changes and you enter the hidden paradise that you painted in your mind's eye.

On the Divine Mode, you will often find that your **Certainty; Absolute Certainty** is being tested, taking you right to the edge. Then suddenly the world opens up.

Learn to handle one target at a time, and map out in days, weeks, months and years, by when the problem must be solved or a change must be made. Have complete certainty that you will get the right message and solution in time. Why worry now, it might never happen; and if it does then you can be sure that if it's good for you the problem will be solved. On the Divine Level, the ultimate light knows what's good for you.

You move ahead and say, 'I don't need to solve that problem for another four weeks. I will have faith that I will get a message and a solution by then'. Why worry now? It might not happen. And so you combine these two, and you go and meditate on this, again, and again

.

This is the time to get your Adrenaline running and to draw down the energy from the Divine

Just Stand-Up and Meditate

Concentrate on the picture on the cover of this book, which is a quiet peaceful forest out in the countryside. You can feel, hear, and almost touch the silence. Now **Stand-Up**, close your eyes, and imagine that you are one of the trees out there in our very private forest.

Now start swaying slowly back and forth, just like a tree in the wind. Pull your head back and push your mind higher and higher. Hold this position for a few minutes. With concentration, you will actually start to feel the force of your Soul and mind standing 'taller and taller'.

In the beginning, you will find it difficult to hold the 'upward' movement and will feel your mind slipping down. Keep focusing on the space high up above your head and concentrate on just pushing up.

Sway back and forth, back and forth ever so slowly like a tree in the wind. This will help you to connect with your Soul. Now start drawing down energy from the Divine Mode. Open your hands, palms upwards, stretching out from the sides of your body. Receive the energy forces generated from the Divine.

Concentrate on receiving the energy , feel your hands starting to get warmer. Concentrating on the upward movement, the swaying, and receive the downloaded energy into the palms of your hands; **repeat this exercise**.

Every Soul
is granted at least one Soulmate,[20]
a reflection of themselves – a twin
They will find each other
no matter what, or where
from distant places, other dimensions
Soon they are communicating
through the language of the Soul
Breathing together and bonding
together in total harmony

Eliyahu Kelman

Chapter Seven

The Most Important Meditation of Your Life

- *Find Meaning in Life… and Deepen Relationships*

- *Removing friction, bringing peace and harmony into your life*

- *All about bonding with those close to you*

- *Breathe together, Bond and stay Together*

This journey is moving us forward and towards achieving what we set out to do right from the beginning. That is to live a life abundantly and fully on the Divine Mode. It has been a tough journey so far, but know now that the ultimate goal will be both rewarding and spectacular.

This journey can be equated to climbing a very steep mountain, every now and again stopping and resting to enjoy the beautiful panoramic views, before moving on again. You must take the opportunity to absorb more knowledge and deepen your understanding through using the **Spaced-Repetition** technique, which will help you to learn and to meditate. You will find the need, as we climb higher, to meditate more and more.

That is why this chapter is a very, very important stage in our self-programming on the Divine Mode. We could not have done this earlier because we had to build an understanding and go through the preparation stages. Now is the time for each of us to work on defragmentation of our mind, our brain's computer. We have to fill in the missing spaces, much like the defrag process runs on your computer.

As you know that takes time and patience. A computer, much like our brain, is constantly moving files around as the information needed changes, new data is acquired and older information filed away. To get these files back in an orderly fashion, a defragmentation is necessary or the computer will run slowly and inefficiently. The same applies to our brilliant brains.

Now as you may know, de-fragmentation works best when nothing else is happening. The process of defragmentation in our brains, in our minds, allows us to clean up our memory and remove from our minds what was previously programmed on the **Default Mode**. What we need to do is to work on activating the software already buried deep within our brain. This will trigger off the ability to move up to the Divine Mode more easily. The process of clearing out the muddle of files in our minds will allow us to utilize the many applications in our brain on a more efficient level, the Divine level.

That is what we have to do right now. And, that is why the whole of this chapter is devoted to meditation.

As with all of your Self-Hypnosis moments, as you have been practicing at the end of each chapter, you need to make yourself comfortable. Find a space in a quiet room, a place where you know you won't be disturbed. But this time I want you to be with your wife, husband or life-long partner. If you do not have a partner at this point in your life, then ask a very close friend or family member to join you.

It will be more effective if you don't do this alone. Do this together with someone close to you.

As mentioned before, the words for soul and breathing in biblical Hebrew are actually quite similar. For a soul it is 'Neshamah' and for breathing it is 'Nishmat hayyim', 'The Breath of Life' The soul comes from the Divine breath that was breathed into the body of Adam, the first man, 'the breath of life' as it were. That is where the Soul came from.

Naturally we have to learn more about those origins but right now, we just need to know how to trigger off the communication between our Souls. The Sages pointed out to us, many years ago, that when couples learn to kiss each other, or parents and children kiss and hug each other, we are essentially breathing in each other's neshamah. This is how soul mating develops[20].

Again, I would like reiterate…

People who
breathe together,
bond together,
and in the end
stay together

Breathing together means staying together

The secret of relationship bonding with those people that we are living and working with, is to breathe together.

There are many well-known stories of prisoners where the captor and captured are thrown together in close contact. Prisoners and jailers, when living in such close quarters, often gradually bond together and eventually come to support each other, slowly developing a relationship. There is oft times an interplay between the Stockholm and Lima Syndromes, where the captured becomes fixated on their captor, often falling in love with them. Alternatively, the opposite occurs, where the captor falls for their prisoner. Most times this results in outcomes not necessarily to the liking of the instigators or the families of the two parties.

Many a prison psychologist, well aware of the power of this breathing factor, will insist on regular changing of the guards, thereby eliminating the risk of a bond forming between the prisoner and jailer.

Even people who have been through times of great stress together, whether in war, during life threatening events, or maybe confined together for long periods of time will experience a bonding process. They will, after bonding, do anything for their bonded mate, anything…

Let us take it a step further. What about school dorms, especially in boarding schools, colleges, universities, anywhere where people breathe together day and night, they too can form strong bonds with each other.

From doing their homework, studying and researching. Together, they can bond for the rest of their lives.

Consider a person graduating from a great University, possibly Harvard, Oxford, Cambridge, the Grande Eçoles of

France; there are many…, they become part of a loyalty network, and most times these networks become their centre of influence, helping them when going forward in their business or personal lives.

But what is the magic behind all of this?

It is so simple. It is in the breathing together.

Now, we have to breathe together as that is the whole point of this meditation exercise. And that is why I suggested your partner or close friend joins you in this experience.

Whenever you have a problem or a challenge, do exactly what we are going to do together right now. This will enable you to relax, to get rid of the tension of the day and essentially separate yourself from the pressures of life on the **Default Mode**. Do this right and you will experience a feeling of well-being and love for each other and everything around you. All your challenges will slip away.

Let us get started.

Sit with your chosen partner for this exercise; and breathe your way through it. If one of you feels comfortable and confident, you could even talk through the meditation together, imagining the scenery as described in the transcripts below.

Start by breathing very slowly, bringing your breathing together in tandem

- Breathe in deeply, fill your lungs up, and then very, very slowly exhale

- Now let do it again - inhale, fill your lungs slowly

- And breathe out – again very slowly

- In and then out - in and then out

- Your breathing in and out should be very slow, paced regularly, making sure you breathe in synchronization with each other

- Keep this up - In, out, in, out…

- Follow the breathing and make sure you hear each other breathing in, breathing out, breathing in, breathing out…

- You have to try to keep this up for ten minutes

- It will seem like you are doing this for ages but eventually you will lose track of all time

- When you get into breathing like this, you will find time, in fact time slows down and you will feel like you are above time, space and motion

- It is quite remarkable. And it is only when you are busy that time seems to fly

- Keep breathing in and breathing out

- Slowly and together breathe in synchronization

- Just imagine you are listening to my voice leading you to breathe in and breathe out slowly

- Conjure in your mind, as you breathe like this, panoramic views of outer space.

- See yourself floating high above planet earth

- Still breathing in and breathing out

- Keep up the slow measured pace. There is no hurry out here

- Breath in - breath out – breath in - breath out

This is the self-programing of your mind, a continuation of what we have been doing together since the beginning of the book. You will start to feel comfortable and relaxed. You will have that 'feel good' sensation percolating throughout your body, your mind and Soul.

After thinking on this for a few minutes, I want you to imagine that you and your partner's Souls have morphed into two birds, flying higher and higher.

Look up and see the panoramic view above.

Look down and see the chaos of the **Default Mode** below.

The two of you are now completely disconnected from all of this on the **Default Mode**. Continue your flight, higher and higher, even into outer space, leaving the earth behind you. As you look back at the beautiful tapestry of the world, marvel at what a wonderful view it is to behold.

- **Keep on breathing in tandem whilst holding these wonderful images in your mind's eye.**

- **Breathing in, breathing out, breathing in, breathing out**

The only thought you must hold in your mind is of your Souls, flying around way out into space - on and on and on.

There is no end to space as there is no end to the ocean [21]. It just goes on, out into infinity, for that is where your Soul really belongs.

All of your problems and challenges lost their importance and have been left behind. The birds, your Souls, have lifted life's baggage from your shoulders. You are just left with the feeling of love between you and all of the Souls in your life, Soulmates flying together.

Now, so very slowly, let your birds fly down from outer space, passing through stunning panoramas, down back into your body and its place in your spacesuit.

Reflect on this experience and remember that …

People who
breathe together,
bond together,
and in the end stay together

When you have repeated this experience several times with your chosen partner, why not enlist your friends and children to join in your next meditation.

Always remember that the key is to breathe in synchronization together. This is the only way you can create an atmosphere of calm, love and relaxation.

Eventually you will find yourselves thinking the same thoughts as those that you meditate with. As the sensation of breathing together develops, you will find a bonding and blending between you and those around you.

Successful marriages and close friendships are built though breathing together; gradually you sense what the others are thinking or about to say. Even if thousands of miles apart there will be a strong and ongoing telepathic connection.

I am sure you have experienced that feeling before, where you sensed the need to just pick up the phone and talk to someone close. We feel when something is wrong and we sense when something is right, when there is happiness or news to share.

As with an onion, remove the layers, layer-by-layer, reaching down to the very core of our Souls.

This way, we stay on the Divine Mode, which is the deeper significance of this meditation exercise.

You may well ask, 'What about those families where the bonding breaks loose and falls apart? What happened to the assurance of positive results when breathing together? What happens when relationships fall apart? What about them?'

It would be natural for you to ask these very relevant and pertinent questions.

When breathing together we sense when something is wrong. When a partner is being unfaithful through thought, word or deed; breathing together with someone else, bored or no longer sincere in their interest; you will sense the weakening of the bond and leading to a gradual breaking of the connection.

The effect of breathing together goes haywire, a constant tension builds in the air and you find you are no longer really breathing together. These are the first signs that one of the partners is experiencing a conflict in their mind. It will be picked up in this meditation exercise.

Watch out for the signs,
follow the feeling
Be open with your partner,
denial seems appealing
Facing reality is the way towards healing
Try to understand what is at fault,
don't leave it alone, nip it in the bud
It's worth fighting for as long as you should
If it's time for a change…
Accept!
It's all for the good

Eliyahu Kelman

Now get your Adrenaline running and draw down the energy from the Divine

Just Stand-Up and Meditate

Concentrate on the picture on the cover of this book, which is a quiet peaceful forest out in the countryside. You can feel, hear, and almost touch the silence. Now **Stand-Up**, close your eyes, and imagine that you are one of the trees out there in our very private forest.

Now start swaying slowly back and forth, just like a tree in the wind. Pull your head back and push your mind higher and higher. Hold this position for a few minutes. With concentration, you will actually start to feel the force of your Soul and mind standing 'taller and taller'.

In the beginning, you will find it difficult to hold the 'upward' movement and will feel your mind slipping down. Keep focusing on the space high up above your head and concentrate on just pushing up.

Sway back and forth, back and forth ever so slowly like a tree in the wind. This will help you to connect with your Soul. Now start drawing down energy from the Divine Mode. Open your hands, palms upwards, stretching out from the sides of your body. Receive the energy forces generated from the Divine.

Concentrate on receiving the energy , feel your hands starting to get warmer. Concentrating on the upward movement, the swaying, and receive the downloaded energy into the palms of your hands; **repeat this exercise**.

*The Soul is delivered factory set
to the Default Mode,
though labelled 'Divine' inside,
gift-wrapped, pre-programmed,
potential beyond Imagination*

*It is for us to activate these apps,
opening up the channels to a direct
communication with the Big Brain*

*A first step towards living above
Time, Space and Motion,*[4]
*leaving behind a world of
chaos and confusion,
uncertainty and hesitation,
to living on the Divine Mode…
The ultimate solution*

Eliyahu Kelman

Chapter Eight

The Power of the Soul on the Divine and the Default Mode

- *Freedom of Choice, embarking on a journey from where you are to where you want to be*

Right throughout the series, the central theme is meditation, or rather Self-Hypnosis. With the addition of **Spaced-Repetition** to our Self-Hypnosis, we will be able to bring about a state of Osmosis, and in turn so reach the Divine Mode.

It is important to program yourself with the continuous background music of the Divine Mode. By background music, I mean the orchestration, which is made up of all the Secrets, rules and insights to the workings of our Souls. It is necessary at all times to live and experience the striving to reach the ultimate goal – The Divine Mode.

There is no other way. You need to be obsessed with the idea and hold it in your mind's eye 24/7. Just as the times when you become obsessed with another person, whether it be for love or infatuation, mimic that behaviour, that same feeling, into this need and have this desire to reach the Divine Mode. Again, through **Spaced-Repetition** and meditation, you are literally reprogramming your brain and your psyche.

I want you to relax in your chair with this book in your hand. I want you to picture what I am telling you, visualize this in your mind. Relax, read and listen to that inner voice as it reacts to the changes that are gradually taking place.

We have to try now to conjure up in our minds the word pictures that I am going to paint for you.

Just think of this scenario

We are witnessing many incidents in this world that do not seem logical when they happen. Good things happening to bad people, almost as if they have special influence with the Divine, if that is even possible, given what we know about the Divine. The opposite seems to happen as well; where the good guys suffer and do not fulfil their dreams in life. There are so many more things happening around us that do not seem to be logical, at least to our limited human way of thinking.

We all wonder, at one time or another, how the Divine thinks, if it is at all possible to use that word on this level.

Think!

Can the Divine even think? Is thinking not a human trait? Does the Divine change its mind from time to time? Why would the Divine change its mind? It runs the world. It is all-powerful. It is everywhere.

On the **Default Mode** most people go through life believing that everything is made up of random events, sheer luck or pure happenstance, with the Divine leaving those people alone to carry on living that way, to just survive and get through life, comfortably or otherwise.

Scientists generally argue with this, saying that the Big Bang was a random event, without taking into consideration what was in existence before, where it came from or how far back it went. Then, and without any real scientific basis for doing so, they theorize that the mathematical questions for life randomly came together at the same time and in the right order.

Now an even more powerful question to ponder: 'How come, out of the billions of different forms of life, just one was given the power to think, to ask questions, to discover, to convey the power of speech, to have emotions, love, fear and the like?

All those people who think scientists are right should bear in mind that there has been no real research or academic proof that of the two ways of thinking, one is right and one is wrong.

'The very line of time begins with the creation event – Matter, energy, time and space - all created in an instant by an intelligent force above space and time. Naturally, the question will come up 'What about the theory of evolution?' We should have no argument with this either way, as it does not really come into the equation. If this is really the way intelligent mankind developed, it still could not have happened without a progressive plan and detailed engineering.

The point is clear; this research bears no relationship to how we live our lives today. We should be extremely careful not to confuse ourselves with these debates and arguments.

Concentrate on where we are, where we would like to be and how we are going to get there

We have an urgent need to create a connection between our inner space, our minds and our souls. Along with these, we must connect with the Big Brain and the Divine, and what this has to offer. What about the question we asked ourselves earlier on? How can we relate our limited understanding to the vastly different set of rules and laws of nature governing the workings of the universe and everything in it, on the Divine Mode?

Most people love cats. They seem to be a smart, deep-thinking kind of animal. They clean and groom themselves and each other, showing us that they are self-sufficient animals. They understand what food to eat and how to ask for food from their human carers. When they feel sick, they make a plan and self-medicate. They purr when they are content and happy, and hiss and howl when they are not. Some cats pay for their keep by chasing mice away, to top it all they even seem to have nine lives.

So, we think they are intelligent, but has anybody examined their brain, probed into their actual level of intelligence, their thought processes? Absolutely not!

So this is my thinking on the matter of cats: Imagine the cat looks at us, and thinks, 'Wow! They're in a different world, these humans, they do not think like us cats. They make these moving machines they call cars. They get married to each other. They have parties. They produce food. These humans do so much. But, I just scrounge for food and for milk. I know how to show these humans when I am hungry by making certain noises, but they work and produce results.

They create so many things that I do not know what to expect next...'

So for the cat, we are thousands, if not a billion miles away in our thought process as opposed to theirs. But, we have no idea what is going on in that little cat's mind, but I surmise he may be thinking...

So just as with this cat story, there is an enormous gulf between our level of intelligence and logic, as related to that of the Divine, which is on a higher plane, a different dimension.

The way we think and understand how things seem to work is just not logical. Take for example travelling into space. We can go on for millions, billions or trillions of miles. Outer space seems endless, when would we reach the end? And even if we did, what would be there, a wall, a river, a stretch of land...

Even more puzzling, what would be on the other side, how far does that stretch is beyond our perception?

If that was not enough, we can ask similar questions about time and history but we would hit the same wall. We just cannot possibly figure it out. This is why I described us living on the Soul level, and the Divine Mode as 'above time, space and motion' where the end as we understand it is endless. Time as we know it is timeless.

So, we have no choice, at this point in our existence, other than to leave the unfathomable alone. How much there is still to discover and understand in this world, just simple things, understanding our wife, or our husband, or even our children who we gave life to, seems an impossible task.

What we need to concentrate on is our own inner space instead of G-d's outer space. An interesting fact about G-d's outer space is that because G-d breathed his Soul into Adam, each and every one of us has G-d inside of us. So, in thinking like that it would mean we, in fact, have 'G-d inside'.

What are the secrets that we have to learn from this? On the **Default Mode**, there are natural processes in the world. People die in accidents.

We cannot explain why a particular person gets killed and not someone else. People die from cancer, some survive. We cannot explain why one got cancer and not the other. Answers to those types of questions are hidden on the Divine Level. So don't try to find the answer here on the **Default Mode**, whilst you are still here on the **Default Mode**. Whatever you are thinking could well be completely off track.

You will never have the answer. You can guess why things happen. Why is it raining today and why will the sun shine tomorrow? It is much the same with trying to understand the Divine. There are so many unanswered questions.

I always say to my family when they complain about nature, 'Wait a minute, are you trying to run G-d's world for Him?' That is exactly what we are trying to do, without thinking.

The best way to describe this is by way of an example. You work very hard on a project, but don't succeed. You just didn't reach the end in time. Or you study for an exam and you don't pass. You study some more but you still don't pass.

The importance in life is in the doing and the way you go about it. It's very interesting that many people make similar plans, really working in the same way, right up until the point where they are ready to commit. One ends in total success and the other in complete failure. The truth: it isn't about success or failure, but other factors beyond our control that are playing out on the great stage of life.

My grandson told me recently that he had been accepted into medical school; but this had taken him three years due to the high level of competition. So keep trying and don't give up. Realise that when you're hoping and praying for something to happen, understand that it might not be for you and that your real path in life is going in another direction. This you need to seek out and discover, remember this and keep going forward regardless.

Don't you have that with your children? When they want something, but you know that giving it to them would be bad for them, you say no.

The same goes for drug addicts; a story comes to mind that I heard from somebody working in a rehabilitation centre. One day he was in discussion with several clients, who had all reached a stage in their treatment where they were due for a break to visit family. He was taken aback when all three told him that they did not want to leave the centre to visit their families; they explained that working with the team had made them feel at home, a real family, mainly because for the first time in their lives they were with people who cared enough to say no.

Everything we have been discussing up to now is really about life on the **Default Mode**. As we progress on our journey of discovery we find that our Soul is all-powerful, and together with the Divine is capable of determining our future.

The big question that most people ask is, 'Well, if my destiny is already mapped out, then where is my freedom of choice?' We all have freedom of choice to choose the way we want to go.

In order to understand this better, let us think of the following scenario, and an important rule

Just imagine
You are about to enter
a Multi-screen Cinema Complex
Buy a ticket,
eight theatres to choose from
You are allowed to get up
in the middle of the film,
walk out and go to another theatre
You have the 'freedom of choice'
to choose between many cinemas
at the same price
That is freedom of choice

The soul in Default Mode
resides in the heart,
two sides fighting
for heart and mind
Material and spiritual,
good or bad,
right or wrong,
which side will win?

The left doomed to a life
on the Default Mode,
the right freed to soar up
towards the Divine Mode.

It's your choice...
you have freedom of choice,
choose any time you're challenged

Eliyahu Kelman

138

Chapter Nine

The Inner Secrets - the two opposing forces programmed into your Soul

- *Listening for messages hidden in people's words and actions; avoiding danger, insincerity and fraud, uncovering opportunities*

- *A time to take action, a time to wait, a time to move forward, even a time to hesitate*

- *When to blow the whistle - when to protect the innocent*

We are still building the stairs to the next floor in our house in the countryside, so that we can get up to the Divine Mode and stay there

At this point, I want to introduce you to the idea of two Souls. Now, it doesn't mean to say that you are occupied by another Soul, not at all. But, it is very interesting that when Souls are described in a human being, it is always in the plural, and when it is in plural, it means there are two. So what does this mean exactly to you? We are told in the ancient writings, the Aggadah, about two Kings[22]... ruling one city ... This is is quite a challenge

Both Kings were fighting continuously to take control of each other's territory and to be the sole King of that city.

Unfortunately, we find this sort of war today in Iraq and Syria, North and South Korea and in many other places throughout the world. That is the way of our world and the way of human nature.

But, here, we are talking about something else. These two Kings waged a marathon struggle to keep control. The difference between the two Kings was that one King was very wicked. He would kill his people without a blink of his eye. He would have them hung for saying something out of turn. He taxed his people heavily in order to satisfy all of his material needs. He was a very arrogant man, and a dictator.

Then we have the other King, a wonderful man. He was like a good, kindly old grandfather. He looked after his people and he tried to help those who were down and out or had difficulties, those who had lost their jobs or suddenly found themselves orphans or widows. Everyone loved that King.

Both Kings struggled to win control of the city. But, as it is with most of my stories, there is always an analogy. So, where is the city? The city is within you, me and every human being on this planet, Earth. The city is our body, trying to work with our mind, our heart and trying to get the actual physical aspects working properly. What you look at, what you hear, what you say and what you are willing to do, are examples of what the body controls.

Now, think of it like this - both Kings are trying to take control of your body. One King is the good Soul or the good inclination, and the other King is that bad Soul, the bad inclination. There is a continuous fight between the two to take control of your body.

So you may ponder and ask why we have such very cleverly created human bodies and why there are so many brilliant parts to our body? There is the brain, but what about the rest of the body? The repair systems, the little factories that operate inside us, managing and running all of our organs. Why do we need two Souls?'

It is incredible how our bodies work. I could go on and on analysing part by part of the fantastic way our body is engineered and built.

But the question must be answered. Why was it engineered with two Souls? It is part of what we talked about in our previous chapter and that is the freedom of choice. But what exactly does 'freedom of choice' mean? You can choose the good King or the bad King. But beware because they know how to trick you. They know how to lead you on and they both know how to take control of your mind. They will offer you all kind of things that look good, that look attractive and which you cannot resist. Think of the Kings as that little devil and little angel, sitting on your shoulders, playfully bantering away, confusing you to the point of frustration. So why do we have these two Souls, tempting us? It is very simple. Nobody achieves anything unless they fight for it. Nobody is born moral or immoral. Yes, they have a tendency to go either way. The family we are brought up in or the society that we live in all play a part in how we will morally run our lives. But at the end of the day, you have to decide when that opportunity comes to steal, cheat, lie or do anything that is considered bad, whether you will or you won't.

You have to resist even if you are starving. There are principles in life and those principles you must adhere to. When you leaning towards the evil inclination and the bad

Soul, you will have a problem, because it will turn around and say, 'Look, what are you worried about? If you don't like these principles, I have other principles for you'.

Now, it might sound a bit funny, but there are people who work like that. They adjust their morals according to their need and you have to beware of that type of person. You simply cannot rely on them. That is why I have one attitude in life. If somebody doesn't keep positive, or has difficulty in believing, that is fine. But if they are agnostic and try to turn anti-religion into a religion in of itself, then that person cannot be trusted. They certainly have principles, but when you don't like those principles then you should avoid that person altogether.

The evil inclination is there for you to use as leverage for good. It sort of strengthens your determination and helps you up to the Divine Mode level.

Better use your freedom of choice to do good.

And, how do you do good? After all none of us are robots.

So, if we are given a challenge and we make the correct decision to do what is right, it is the evil inclination that forced you in that direction in the first place. If you didn't have to make a decision, then there would be no evil Soul.

Just imagine what it will be like if when we are born into this world, we don't have to lie, we don't know how to lie. We don't have to do things wrong. We don't even know how to cheat, how to steal or how to commit adultery.

So, what is the big deal? Why are we born in the first place? G-d could just as well have put robots in this world, because that is what you would have become. So, because freedom of choice is so precious, you are given that other side to try to pull you all the time to the golden mean, the middle path between right and wrong, good and bad.

I would like to give you the example of Maimonides[23], one of the leading commentators, philosophers and doctors of his time, five centuries ago. Well-known in Spain, he also served as the medical advisor to the Grand Vizier in Egypt.

He proposed the following school of thought: What was the difference between the time when Adam and Eve were inside the Garden of Eden, and when Adam and Eve left the Garden of Eden? During the brief era of the Garden of Eden, they knew that everything was black or white, right or wrong. When they were expelled from the Garden of Eden, then everything had its own rationale, a sort of dark grey shadow in between. 'Well, it is not so bad but it is not so good either'.

And this is how we see things today, well most of us. If it is pretty near to being all right then it is Okay. We are all aware of the type of people who try to make excuses for their behaviour, who always try to seek out a justification for doing what they want to do, regardless of the moral or legal issues involved. They give themselves permission to do something, which is inherently wrong.

I have very close colleagues who only see the world in black or white.

They have no tolerance for anything else. That is sometimes very difficult, because one needs to be tolerant of other people. You can set your standards high, but you have to expect that other people are still going through the fight between the two Kings. We are all given an opportunity to move up to the other grade, until it becomes part of our life and automatic way of thinking.

Another famous philosopher, Rabbi Dessler[24] said something powerful and worthwhile remembering:

> *'Everybody has their own level of truth.*
> *People do not necessarily lie,*
> *but they do have*
> *their own particular level of truth'.*

We must bear this in mind; try to understand where they are coming from and what drives them. You do not necessarily have to accept them and go along with what they have decided to do, but it will do you well to know how these people think.

People do not lie and cheat intentionally, unless they are basically wicked. You can recognise them easily.

They simply create their own level of truth.

What we do on the **Default Mode** is to treat people and opportunities that come our way to a dose of our own level of truth and we do not compromise. On the Divine Mode, the way we are going to build these steps brick by brick is to gradually notch up our level of truth.

We need to make our level of truth closer to that of the Divine, far away from the level that is acceptable on the **Default Mode**.

I would like to take you back to another story that comes to my mind, but just fits into what we have been talking about here.

A number of years ago, quite early in my career, during the time when I was running training courses for the management of large companies; I would hire myself out, effectively as a timeshare managing director pro-tem, a guide to companies. I would take on positions within their organisations in order to get a project launched.

Authors are generally advised to refrain from disclosing real names of individuals, companies and institutions, occasionally even the name of the country where the story took place, this serves to protect the privacy of the indivduals involved.

My job came with dream terms and conditions, including generous bonuses, to be the stand-in Managing Director until the company would be ready to appoint a permanent Director. The company operated in the timeshare development business, building apartment hotel resorts and then selling off slices of time in the apartments to investors. If you want to know more, just Google it, you will have the whole explanation in seconds, so I won't spend time going into an explanation here.

The end result was that they sold off the apartments in the hotel, but retained effective ownership; in addition their upfront capital gains were very significant.

The company was able to charge for the general running of the timeshare operation on behalf of the purchasers. As you can imagine, this was a very attractive scheme. I had in the past worked for a major international player who was doing this all over the world.

So, here I was in a position, a uniquely strong position, because the Board of Directors actually informed both the

Bank and everyone we were dealing with that anything that I said needed to be done must be treated as though the Board of Directors had made the decision to do so themselves. Essentially they granted me that right and everyone involved received confirmation of this decision in writing.

I couldn't have worked in any other way on this particular project. The main job was really to organise their sales and to do it internationally, because this was a very big project, at that time one of the largest timeshare projects worldwide, in all selling some 15,000 individual units.

Now, in the early days when trust laws were vague, the sellers had to find a way to satisfy the purchasers need for a sense of security whilst the building was being constructed.

The hotel was being built with the timeshare unit owners' money. They had to make sure that they were fully covered.

In order to satisfy this need the company announced that they would establish a Trust account. All of this had been orchestrated before I became an advisor to the company.

All the investors money was to be held in a Trust account, only being transferred to the sponsors when the hotel was completed and handed over to the timeshare owners. Normally, and for any promotion today, it would be required by law to have a full disclosure of the the Trust operations, including the rights and obligations of all Parties; however at that time the laws were simply not in place.

And so, I came in with great enthusiasm for this wonderful group of people. I enjoyed working with the executive board. I organised teams to go out and sell and within a short period success seemed assured. The sales started to came in and it was quite incredible to watch.

Now, I don't know what got into my head, but one day, I decided to sit down with the Bank to find out how the Trust was doing. This was the first message that I received from the Divine level. It came through when someone asked me, 'How much money is in the Trust today? How much have you sold? Do you know how the Trust works? 'Look I'm a lawyer and I know there are no trust laws. So, how can you have a Trust?' I had to treat this as a message download from the Divine Mode. The warning bells were ringing loud and clear. Never, ever ignore messages; I didn't that time, and I was very pleased that I didn't. I went to see the Bank and asked to see the Trust accounts.

The Account Manager's face went white and of course this sign I didn't miss. He stumbled over his words and eventually said: 'I can't show you that. It's private information belonging to the owners of the company'.

'My dear friend, I can see on your face why you don't want to show me. Now, listen to me very, very carefully. You have clear instructions from the Board of Directors of the company that anything I ask for or want to do must be treated as if a decision was made by the Board of Directors themselves. Don't even think of lifting up the phone and talking to them, because if I do find something out, it means that you are part of the scheme of things'.

I knew where I stood by his reaction, it was clear that the messages that were streaming into my mind were showing me which way this was going. So, I continued, 'You make your decision. It's your career. Right now, you are running an account and you are not obligated under trust law, but the minute I ask you then you are obligated under the transparency act, which does not allow you to withhold sensitive information of this nature. Withholding any information means that you are part of it'.

He reluctantly showed me the accounts, which were almost completely empty. The people building the time-share hotel were also major real estate developers; it was clear that the ring-fenced funds held in Trust for the timeshare owners were being used to fund their other developments.

In other words, unbeknown to the purchasers who thought their money was safely held in a Trust, it was being used to finance an enormous real estate business, all in addition to the hotel that was being built. They were all exposed to the inherent risk in the developer's other highly leveraged businesses. Had the company not declared that the money was being held in trust then incoming deposits and payments would have belonged to the builders to do with what they liked. Selling under false pretences as to the level of security offered made the whole transaction fraudulent, even though there was no trust law as such.

I looked him directly in the eyes and said:

'I want you to forget we had this conversation. I don't want you to talk to anybody. Leave it alone. I want to think about what I am going to do now'.

Now you would have thought, as an upstanding citizen, that I should have gone immediately to report this to the police'. But, I thought to myself, 'Wait a minute. I have a responsibility to the buyers as well. They could be seriously damaged'. I thought this over very carefully. To have gone to the police would have shut down the company and thousands of people would have lost their money, not to mention the loss of jobs within the company. Buyers wouldn't have had a chance to recover their investment at all. The only way was to make them continue on their building project, but with every penny that was coming in being immediately deposited into the trust account, where it belonged.

Remember this, in life; everybody thinks that in modern society it is a moral duty to report, to blow the whistle. However one must always weigh up the consequences.

Never forget this cardinal rule:

'You cannot be a righteous person at the expense of other people'

I do not mean that if somebody commits a felony, steals or is dishonest, that you shouldn't report it, that you shouldn't stop it in its tracks. No, I didn't mean that at all. What I mean is that you have to be very careful that you do not act like a terrorist. You might think that you are perfectly justified in throwing a hand grenade at the person who is leading the wickedness in society, but remember; all sorts of innocent bystanders surround him too. We worry about the innocent bystanders who get killed in the supermarket or on the road, so why not the innocent people caught up in connection with a fraudulent scheme?

I must reiterate that I am not justifying what they did. Most of us would not agree with their way of action. But the people who are doing it really think that they are justified and that they are not wrong. What should stop them is all these innocent bystanders being maimed or killed. I had no intention of acting like a terrorist at that juncture in my life.

However, no matter how wrong it was, I knew that reporting it would lead to arrests, a liquidation, and then what…? Lawyers would have taken over, gobbling up the lions share. Assets would have been sold for a song to friends or contacts of the liquidators. I know that I am ruffling the feathers of honest and upstanding citizens, but that is the truth. I had made up my mind. My first duty was to safeguard the investors. It wasn't as if we had no solution to save the company.

In brief, this is what happened. I went to the Board of Directors. I told them what I had found out. I said, right now, there was going to be an independent trust. I told them that we were not going to tell the Trustees what happened, but that they were going to gradually sell their properties and put the money back into the trust.

I did tell them they had a choice, with a built in 'no choice'. I organised it for them and the minute I finished, having taken a few months, I walked away. I could have sued them for compensation, for millions, but I didn't.

They would have had to pay me a lot of money, but I was not going to get involved in bribery. That, in effect, was what it would have been. That cost me a lot of money, but I walked away. I didn't even call them, I didn't even resign. I had nothing to do with them, even when they tried for months to get hold of me because they still had to run the company. They sent friends. They sent all sorts of contacts to me and I didn't even explain to anybody why I wouldn't talk to them. I just said, 'I am not interested any more. I don't want to work with them'. Now, that was an enormous challenge. I wonder how many people could **Stand-Up** to that. Well, I had an advantage, I had been on the Divine

Mode for many, many years by then; everything was crystal clear to me.

> *'I am the master of my fate.*
> *I am the Captain of my Soul'*

William Ernest Henley

Remember this rule:

> *Everything is either*
> *black or white*
> *That is the difference between*
> *right and wrong,*
> *there should be no grey shadow*
> *in between*

You might say, 'But what you did was in the grey area'. Oh no, it was not. Because of the people who would have been affected, the wrong done against them was clearly in the black and my obligation was clearly in the white.

That was my decision to take, and so I took it. I do not say that you should, but you must not worry about giving up a job, closing your eyes to fraud within a company. You don't have to necessarily blow a whistle as people do, harming many shareholders and as a result lose a lot of money. You don't necessarily have to do it. Even though sometimes, you could be punished by law for not doing so. If there is a price you have to pay, you pay it. So that is how you have to weigh up the decision making process. That is being on the Divine Mode. Ignoring completely everything else, doing

the right thing even though it means you would have
difficulty in putting food on the table for your own family.

You cannot live on
'Bread of Shame' [25]

Using money and working for people who are wrong,
wicked, illegal, and dangerous, that would include drug
dealers and smugglers, but also include all sorts of very
respectable, well-dressed people, but it still includes them.

Not giving society a fair return on what society gives you,
unless of course, G-d forbid, you are ill, crippled, or very
old. If you have no other way of doing it then fair enough,
but if at all possible always avoid the bread of shame.

So, what do you think I did after that? How did I survive? I
was lecturing at night and then hitchhiking home because I
couldn't afford the transport. I gave up on sleep and worked
eighteen hours a day. I wasn't ashamed to do so as I did not
want to live on bread of shame.

Don't avoid the issue by putting your 'Hand across your
heart' and declaring that these were your beliefs and level of
truth. Live them. It is very hard. It is very difficult and many
times, people around you might look at it differently. But
when you are on the Divine Mode, you only have one
responsibility - what's that responsibility? It's the purity and
the clarity of your Soul.

Now we have reached the time when we must meditate on
everything that we have learned today. Let us go up to our
favourite place, where we have to use our imagination. I
want you to relax. I want you to slow down. I want you to
cut out all interference. I want you to think of the instances

in your lives when you have given up on principles, when you have done the wrong thing. When you have closed your eyes and looked the other way. When you were thinking, 'Well, I'm not involved... I am just a very small cog in a big wheel'. Don't kid yourself. However small it is, you are still part of the wheel and it affects your Soul.

If you ever have a problem with the difference between black, white and shades of grey, think about what your children would say if they knew who you really were. I am not talking about you doing it directly. I am talking about living a life of convenience. Examine yourself deeply. Look yourself in the eye and say, 'Am I doing the right thing?'

Now, many of you will say and quite rightly so, that it doesn't apply to you. But I will tell you where it does apply. Each one, each Soul is responsible for another Soul. The question was asked by Nachman of Breslev[26] and I have mentioned him before. Hundreds of years ago, this great man, very poor, kind and wise, liked to state his rule for life:

'Why is a Soul born?
It is to do a favour for someone else'

And how do you translate that favour? It is not just giving him a gift and helping him out. It is much more than that. It is helping him to avoid pitfalls. So you point out to colleagues in a diplomatic fashion, very privately, 'Watch it. What you are doing is cutting corners. If small actions affect your Soul, how much more do the big ones?

If you say it,
you can create it and like magic
it will happen as you speak
Abra-Ca-Dabra

Chapter Ten

Conflict Resolution in your personal life

- *Turning the impossible into the possible - participate in the control of events*

- *An impossible adventure; demonstrating the Codes of Life in action*

As the title of the chapter suggests, we must work together to keep you heading towards the Divine Mode, no matter what level you have managed to reach up to now, it really doesn't matter which level you are on. There is no rush. It is, in fact, better not to rush.

In order to keep on track towards the Divine Mode, we need to go straight to Self-Hypnosis, we never stop with meditation. Hopefully by now you are more efficient in getting yourself into the right meditation mood and are able to conjure up the images that we have created in the past.

Before you make yourself comfortable and settle down in an easy chair, prepare yourself, with all sounds that might interfere blocked out of your mind.

We need to set the tone by Going back to the '**Stand-Up** meditation' earlier in the book (see p10).

This is important to help you Internalize the thoughts, rules and secrets, so making the way of living on the Divine Mode the only way to go.

Put yourself on 'automatic pilot'.

We are going up above all the distraction and chaos on the **Default Mode**; we are going up into outer space again.

One has to see where you have come from, in order to know where you are going. Always bear this in mind, throughout your relationship with other people and with yourself...

Certainty, Absolute Certainty

The following real life story, will illustrate this rule when combined together with its natural working partner, **Abra-Ca-Dabra**.

Whenever you are facing difficult challenges just remind yourself of the following -

Certainty, Absolute Certainty,
together with the force of Abra-Ca-Dabra
Brings the impossible into
the realms of reality

You have to have the confidence and talk only positively. No negativity.

No negative talk whatsoever.

The Divine will create for you as you speak, and because it is you who speaking the **Abra-Ca-Dabra**.

So, let us get on with our story.

The scene takes place in New York, quite some time back. It was just before Thanksgiving Day and I had completed a marathon session of meetings, three days of negotiations, day and night.

For the benefit of those who have never been in the United States over the Thanksgiving period, there is one basic rule, and that is to avoid travelling over the holiday weekend.

The whole of America is on the move and complete chaos reigns. Flights and trains are overbooked or delayed, pretty much playing havoc with everyone's schedules. The roads are gridlocked and rental cars have all been solidly booked months ahead. Everybody is under great pressure to get to their destinations and the hassled airport staff work hard to make it all happen.

You must be smart in order to stay ahead of the game in New York, never mind over Thanksgiving.

Having never experienced this, I did not know what to expect, until one of my friends gave me a warning and some sound advice. 'The most important thing is to be prepared for all eventualities. You can be hit with traffic delays just getting to the airport. The airlines overbook in order to keep themselves covered and offer all sorts of attractive freebies to persuade customers to give up their seats and delay their departure to the next flight'.

So, while I couldn't avoid travelling over this Thanksgiving time, I took his advice to heart, I wanted to make sure that I got back to my daughter and grandchildren in Boston on time. I bought two tickets, with a gap of a few hours between flights, and made sure that they were both business class. This way I was covering myself in the event of missing the first flight. Extravagant, but a necessary evil, I thought.

Well, there I was in the taxi. I had finished my meetings and was heading for La Guardia airport. Even though I had allowed many hours more than necessary for this trip, I knew it could still be extremely busy and frustrating.

I was very tired, so instead of watching the traffic and mentally driving for the chauffeur, I took my package of traveller's checks, passport and tickets, put them next to me between my seat and the driver's, and fell asleep.

Suddenly I heard the driver tell me that according to the time, the plane should be just taking off. I told him not to worry about it as I had Absolute Certainty that I would fly. Naturally, **Abra-Ca-Dabra** was now very much in play, that was how I always spoke and how I really felt. The driver couldn't follow my logic, so he did not respond.

I paid the taxi driver and got out of the cab, took my luggage and started to run. As I entered the airport I suddenly realised, 'Wow! I've left my tickets, my passport and traveller's checks, all behind in the cab… What am I going to do?'

The Cabbie was already moving off, although I waved to him, the only response was his tail lights vanishing into the distance. What do you do? I knew I had to act fast.

Then I noticed that there was another taxi letting off a passenger at arrivals. Even though I knew that he was not allowed to pick up any passengers before returning to the taxi rank and wait his turn, I went over to him, and said, 'Look, I will give you $200 if you chase after that taxi. We have to stop him as I have left all my important documents on his back seat. The cabbie answered me with a very surprised face, 'You're absolutely crazy. You're throwing away your money - $200 was a lot of money in those days, more equivalent to around $600 or $700 now.

He was adamant there wasn't a chance and said as much.. 'There are 20 taxi ranks. He is going to one of those ranks where he will wait his turn. Each rank has 500 taxis and they all look the same. How do you expect to find him? This really is a needle in the haystack'.

I answered him with confidence and Absolute Certainty, 'We will find him and anyway I have no choice. Without my passport, traveller's checks and tickets I am stuck here. Everyone must have faith and right now this is all that we can work on. We will get it back, we will celebrate and I will fly'.

'How are you going to be able to manage that? Your flight is taking off right now...'

I answered again with confidence, 'I will fly'.

So we zoomed off and soon found ourselves cruising past the first taxi rank, moving slowly down the line to see if I could recognize the driver… No driver.

We moved then to the second taxi rank and did the same. As you would expect, the taxi driver reiterated his frustration, 'This is an exercise in futility'.

So, I patiently said, 'My dear friend, you have to have absolute belief. Otherwise, nothing will happen'.

Finally, we reached the sixth rank and somehow in the haze I recognised my driver lolling next to his cab. They were all yellow cabs so there was no way to recognize the difference between each one, but I recognised him. We pulled alongside and I got out of the taxi. When I opened his back door, he was, of course, quite surprised to see me.

I smiled and said, 'You hadn't noticed this, had you?' And I bent down to pick up the valuable package, thanking G-d that it was still intact.

I took it firmly in my hand, went back to my second Cabbie and said to my driver, 'Come, we go back'.

We finally returned to the terminal an hour and a half after my flight had taken off. I asked the driver to park his cab and join me to witness what happened next. We looked up at the Departures Board to see that the flight I had missed had in fact been delayed. We approached the check-in desk and presented my ticket to the agent…

'Sorry, you didn't come on time, so I have given away your place'.

My immediate response was, 'You had no right... I bought that ticket and booked the place, so you really had no right to give it away'.

Her response...? 'Sorry sir, we are not obligated to wait for you. The law clearly states that even if the plane has not yet taken off, I am allowed to give away your place if you haven't checked in at least 30 minutes before the flight'.

'Can't you do anything for me?' I pleaded.

'Sorry, we are overbooked and I cannot put you on the next flight either, or even the flight after that, as they are also fully booked'.

'Good... I am one of the people who booked'.

When I produced my second ticket, she was absolutely shocked and surprised, but in a way a little bit pleased for me too. And so, she checked me in..., and I still had a 20 minute wait when I finally got to the departure lounge. It was unbelievable.

The taxi driver had been so emotional when we arrived at the airport and had said, 'Never in my life have I met somebody like you. You have actually done the impossible'.

'My dear friend, I have not done the impossible. I simply believed absolutely that we would find that taxi driver and we would make it'.

I explained **Abra-Ca-Dabra** to him on the spot. Even though he was Catholic and religious, he had been quite taken aback with what I had to say.

'You have to believe in the Divine. You have to have certainty and then and only then will you get things done. We all experience miracles at some point or another in our lives but we have to help to create them. Always bear that in mind. That is why it is worthwhile being up here on the Divine Mode. And you know what? It is a terrific experience'.

The driver answered with a sheepish smile, 'Well, it is Thanksgiving, so I do go to church, but I don't spend much time there. However for the first time I am going to go with my whole family to church and we are going to celebrate because we have to thank G-d'.

'You should. You got the $200'.

'Yes and I'm taking my family out for the best Thanksgiving dinner they have ever had in their lives. And I'm going to tell them this story whether they believe it or not'.

That was a fantastic story, wasn't it? Even when I look back, I get a feeling of joy and goose bumps whenever I tell it.

I have many more fantastical stories. And, as we move along, this adventure will get more and more exciting. It took me many, many years to get up onto the Divine Mode. And what happened as I reached that level; I moved forward and filled my life with **Abra-Ca-Dabra** and Certainty, Absolute Certainty, together with all of the other rules I have told you about and many more to come.

Now, I am living it 24/7. I am literally on automatic pilot today. And what do you think happens when you are on automatic Divine Mode pilot? It attracts an enormous number of fantastical happenstance stories, just like the one I told you now.

The intention of my telling you these stories is to give you be confidence and encourage to say, 'Wow! It's worth it'.

I want you to think about how many times you have been in an impossible situation and didn't have the confidence to even try to get out of it.

The comfort of being on the Divine Mode helps you to realise, slowly, the real meaning of the communication between your tiny little soul and the great Big Soul. It means that on a very much-reduced level, you have the power to do things beyond what you believe could be at all possible and certainly beyond everything that you have been taught before you started reading this book.

Now do you see what I mean when I said it isn't just a case of good ideas on how to succeed? I've been there and I have done that. And I want to share it all with you right here in this book.

My dear friends please carry on going through meditation. Carry on being determined. Carry on with **Abra-Ca-Dabra** and Certainty, Absolute Certainty. And one day you too will be able to relate your own fantastical stories.

I want you to keep in touch; whenever something happens to your life you should share your experiences with me.

It gives me great pleasure each time I see and learn how another person has been helped towards changing their life experiences.

Now, let's continue our meditation and think about the times you could have used this to change the outcome. Just imagine what could have happened if you did?

Once you have finished reading this chapter, close your eyes and imagine yourself in a difficult situation. Just look back in your minds at the various happenstances in your life, those you would love to have changed... Think of the missed opportunities, the times when something beyond your control caused you to lose out in some manner. You may think to yourself, 'If only I had understood what the Divine Mode was all about, or even knew of its possibilities, I could have pulled myself out of the **Default Mode**'.

But you know you have to do the work.

*All I can do is
to knock on the small door
on the outside of your head
You are the only one
who can open it
from the inside*

Meditate on all you have learnt,
think of the times
when you had a thought…
Did nothing about it,
justifying yourself,
not a wise thing to do
Leave the Default Mode behind,
and head up to the Divine
Go forward with
Certainty, Absolute Certainty
and Abra-Ca-Dabra combined

Eliyahu Kelman

Let your radar
pick up every little signal

Listen to the messages
streaming into your mind

Enter a world
of awareness and clarity,
open new levels in your consciousness,
let creativity abound

Eliyahu Kelman

Chapter Eleven

Always have your Radar up and
never Ignore Messages

- *Using Certainty, Absolute Certainty and Abra-Ca-Dabra - turning the impossible into the possible, all wrapped up in one package*

In this session, we are going to talk about messages and how they link to **Abra-Ca-Dabra** and **Absolute Certainty**.

They are always there and act as a backdrop to whatever you learn. **Abra-Ca-Dabra** and **Absolute Certainty** must go hand in hand.

Every now and again, something comes in to your mind, and you wonder, 'Well, if I don't do it now, I may lose out'. Or, perhaps you need to travel but have a bad feeling about making the journey. It could be on a simpler level too, like when you decided not to take your raincoat or umbrella out with you, even though you were receiving a strong message to do so.

But on a higher level, that can become more complicated, if you haven't learned how to recognise the messages, to listen to them, and to act.

On the Default Mode some call it instinct, but where does instinct come from?

Have you noticed that most of the time we start speaking without really knowing what will be voiced next? Each group of three words lead to the next even if we have learned our lines by rote. This is a sure sign of a download from the Divine Mode. We don't think of it that way, but we have all experienced this actually happening.

Many a person has found themselves in front of a crowd and having to give an impromptu speech, or perhaps having planned a speech stood up but then found that we were hitting a complete blank.

Those first three words often come quite suddenly and unexpectedly, catapulting us into the rest of our speech.

A little push,
a little nudge,
is all that it is needed

The Divine is helping us all,
in small, meaningful ways.

Never ignore a sensation…
positive or negative
right or wrong
These are all messages
from the Big Brain
filtering through your soul
into your mind

Just imagine that little voice whispering in your ear, growing ever louder and clearer. If you don't pay attention then, whatever is whispered will gradually fade away, because you are not listening.

Don't we often do that in our relationship with family and friends? If you think that they are not going to listen, you won't bother to talk, after all, what's the point? In reverse, you probably also have times when you don't listen to those close around you and most times miss out on wonderful messages.

Listening, gives us the opportunity of gaining deeper insights into peoples' Souls. So, always listen. No matter, whether to that small voice inside your head, either warning or spurring you on, or to a friend or family member, who may just tell you something very valuable.

And talking about fantastical stories, I have a great story for you, which will explain the combination of messages you need to listen to in order to guard yourself against certain people, those people, who have their hand in your pocket. And at the same time, we will learn more about **Certainty, Absolute Certainty**, and how this can solve any problem facing us.

This story takes us back to New York. At that time, I was consulting for an Investment Bank and working with some of the other well-known Banks in the area. One day I received a call from a company in Albuquerque. If any of you have been to Albuquerque, you will know that Albuquerque is still very much like the old, wild and woolly West, where folk still go out with guns strapped to their hips. They wear stirrup boots and cowboy hats, bars with swing doors still exist. Everything from the Wild West, that's Albuquerque. It's oil country, where they pump oil and dig for other minerals as well. If they are successful, they can make a lot of money.

But it was there that I learned an important lesson from one of the old hands in a big investment company.

Always be careful of
the cowboys of Albuquerque,
the speculators in Vancouver

These people make more money
drilling in the stock exchange
than drilling in the fields
They can tell you anything...
Listen to them very carefully,
analyse!

Trust but Verify

Anon

Well, back to my story. I was responding to a call from an investment company in Canada, who said, 'We want to send our private jet to pick you up and take you to Albuquerque, to see a wonderful investment opportunity'.

So, why refuse? They were paying for my time and the trip, so I was in. The Jet was luxurious; the mile-long limo meeting us at the airport was way out of sight, but none of this had the intended effect on me.

They drove me straight out to the fields, right past the oil wells, to a mineshaft. I was curious, as you can imagine, so I asked, 'Albuquerque is full of oil wells. Everybody's drilling. You can't even bury somebody out here, because oil might spurt out. So, why are you taking me to a mine?'

'We discovered something very interesting. Whilst you are here, we are going to send down the drill bit. It's drilling for oil, but let's see what it comes up with'.

Well, it came up eventually and I was not at all surprised. He got quite excited and lifted out a tiny nugget of gold. With a whoop, this fellow says to me,

'Wow! There is a load of gold down there. Fantastic! We won't need your people's investment after all. We don't need to go on the stock exchange. We're okay'.

Being the gogetter that I was, I decided to call their bluff: 'That's fine, if that is your decision. But, wouldn't you like me to take this gold back and show it to some prominent people I am close to on Wall Street. Let's see how they react'.

'Just go ahead with whatever plan you put together. Naturally, we'll cover your fees, whatever they are'.

Now, I had a gut feeling that the drill had gone down with the gold and had then come up with the same gold. I was so sure in my mind and that message grew stronger and stronger as the day went by. I had no doubt about it.

That was as a direct result of living on the Divine Mode. I was not pulled down or influenced by these people living on the **Default Mode**.

Nevertheless, I didn't say anything. I didn't let on as to what I was thinking.

I said, 'This is real gold. I can feel it'.

They were very happy and drove me straight to the airport, in order that I could catch my scheduled flight back. I had booked my flight to make sure that I arrived in Boston before the Sabbath. It was quite interesting, that once again, I was going to be caught up with another adventure on my way to be with my daughter and grandchildren.

We made it to the airport with plenty of time to spare, at least that's what I thought. But I hadn't realised how big the airport was. And, so I ran and ran. It wasn't easy but at last I arrived at the gate. The booking agent seemed to have the same tale as last time.

'I'm terribly sorry Sir, but you have missed your flight. The doors are closed and the flight will be taxiing out in a few minutes'.

I was quite adamant that I would fly, much like last time, so I said,

'Absolutely impossible! I am willing to spend any amount of money that it will take to get me to Boston on time'.

The agent looked sympathetic, but said, 'Look, you also have to accept reality'.

'I believe absolutely and there is no question about it that I will get there. How I will get there? I don't know. But, I want you to work together with me to help me find how we are going to do it. Believe me; you'll get the biggest box of chocolates you have ever seen in your life if you succeed. …And when you succeed, it will have been out of pure love because that's what you deserve'.

Well, I got away with it as she was young and I was much older. She didn't think I was flirting with her, I wasn't of course, but she turned around to me and said, 'You know my grandfather is a pastor and a very religious man.

He talks exactly like you'

'Great'. I said, 'So, we speak the same language, but don't call your grandfather just yet. Go onto the computer and see what we can do. I don't mind you flying me to Hawaii and back, to get to Boston, I've only got so many hours'.

She would have to look for any combination and I would have to pay whatever the cost would be, because as a person of principles I had to stick to those principles. The client had given me a really good fee for that trip, I was prepared to blow it all, but I was sure that this would not be necessary.

She searched high and low, really trying every possible angle, even flying via Canada. But, there was no way to get me to Boston in good time, even using a combination of two or three flights.

'Look, I can't do any more for you'. She said, with a sad smile.

'My dear, I am flying and that is it'.

She said again, 'But you have to face reality'.

I continued with my positive speak, 'I know that you want to get home as soon as possible, but my home is not here. And you'll see; the plane that taxied out is going to take me now'.

I had no reason to say it, but it came out of my mouth as an automatic download. I heard myself saying this but couldn't control it. It is a strange phenomenon, but that is what happens with direct downloads.

Believe this, or not, just then the phone rang and after listening for a while she looked up, a quizzical expression crossing her face and asked, 'What did you do?'

I frowned and asked her, 'What did I do? I just told you what I believed in'.

So she says, 'One of the cabin crew has fallen ill. They have to turn around and come back. The plane will be at the gate in 20 minutes. It appears I can put you on the plane'.

She was quite emotional and frankly, so was I. I ran off, bought a big, big box of chocolates, and when I got back to her. I took her hands and I told her, 'We are going to dance together, because we have to celebrate. Please tell your grandfather what happened today. It wasn't because I was clever. It was just simply because I knew deep down something was going to happen. I knew that it had to happen. I'm not saying I caused the man to be ill. G-d forbid, I wouldn't think that at all, but you know what, the way it works is like this... Something had to happen, whether it's was a miracle or a happenstance, such as a crewmember being taken ill and being unable to fly.

What was the secret?

It happened at the right time and at the right moment. It could have happened while they were up in the air, too late to return to the gate, but it didn't. Now everybody is going home, it just happened at the right time'.

The booking agent was beside herself with shock and joy, and we did our little jig right there at the gate. It was a surreal and funny moment in my life, and one I will never forget.

We have more power than we believe we have. If it wasn't going to turn out for the good, I would not have received the message of certainty. And if I hadn't listened to that message of certainty, it probably wouldn't have worked out that way either. In other words, the Freedom of Choice was to believe it would happen, or not believe it at all. I was certain it was going to happen, but I was not certain exactly how it was going to happen. And that was OK. Any positive outcome was good with me.

Let's take a look at a scientist. He's sitting there when suddenly a new idea comes into his mind. He has no reason to say he can't do it. As scientists are, he will be trapped into an obsession that he must investigate and research deeper. There will be frustration, hard work, dogged determination, many setbacks, but he just carries on, working through adversity; and all being well, eventually to find that which he is looking for.

Where does it come from? Where is the logic behind it? It is simple. The thought or the message would not have come into his mind if it were impossible to achieve. Why him? Again, that is what was meant to be.

Flashes from the Divine Mode

As we come to the end of this chapter, and after those amazing stories, let us meditate on this important lesson we have learnt.

Let the ideas flow and remember that any crazy thought that comes into your mind, would only be received because it was possible. Think right back into the past. Is there anything out there that you ignored and didn't follow through on? Possibly a career decision, perhaps it was the solution to a problem, a new idea or way of doing something. Maybe it was a relationship decision; perhaps a new invention, a musical score, a new device or software idea.

No matter what it was just remember this:

Always keep your radar up,
look out for messages,
just never forget…
When the Impossible seems Possible
The thought is only there
because it can be done,
otherwise,
it would simply not be there

Eliyahu Kelman

Meditate on all you have learnt,
think of all the times
when you had a thought
Doing nothing about it,
but every time justifying yourself…
Not a wise thing to do…
Leave the Default Mode behind,
reach up to the Divine
with Certainty Absolute Certainty
and Abra-Ca-Dabra combined

Abra-Ca-Dabra
As I speak, I will create
As I create, I will speak

Our mind
is like a stained glass window,
the picture is there, but not clear

Go into your inner space,
turn on the lights,
watch the panorama open up…
The message is there

The Eureka moment arrives…
Everything becomes clear,
you have the answer,
you have the idea.

Eliyahu Kelman

Chapter Twelve

Within the Codes of Life are hidden the Inner Secrets of Downloading Messages

- *Listen – Then understand*

- *Seeing ahead through chaos, denial, fraud, lies, greed and downright stupidity*

- *Navigating by reading ahead, before the great crash of 2008*

In the last chapter we learnt how to combine **Certainty, Absolute Certainty** with **Abra-ca-Dabra**. We finished that chapter with a thought about messages. Now we are going to learn about how to download messages, listen to messages, recognise them, and act on them. This is where the Big Brain and your little brain take on important roles.

So, sit back and relax. Be ready. Make a condition with yourself that you will be determined to absorb everything. This will enable you to gradually open up the channels and recognise messages. You will then take notice of them and they will become ever stronger as you go forward.

We are going to move through this chapter with meditation again. In this meditation, I want you to imagine that you are up in space. Up here you can see the mass of the universe that makes up the Big Brain. Keep in your mind the fact you are looking at everything through your inner universe, which is the same for every human being.

Each and every person has their own level of consciousness, developed over time. This is your task throughout. To continually think, develop and program your mind to be able to tap into all the potential, which lies hidden within your own inner self. There is such an enormous difference between the Big Brain and everything it contains, and your brain, which is only limited to each person's area of interest. You are only tapping into a very small part of this vast bank of knowledge and information. Unfortunately, most humans only ever use about 2% of the potential data space available in their brains, sad, but true. Here, I will try to help you to utilise more than that 2%.

Just remember that all of the messages that are streaming into your mind are specific to your needs and requirements, which will enable you to be the 'You'. the entity that you are meant to be. All of these messages will be mixtures of clear pictures, hints and ideas, normally in step-by-step parts. All are clever, mysterious, sometimes in code, and often revealing themselves fleetingly, leaving you trying to figure them out on your own.

Your brain is continuously downloading solutions and warnings about people, ideas and plans. The messages are there for you to heed, to caution you or to spur you on to do something. In time, this becomes an automatic way of life and living.

Everyone starts off with a good Soul, who loves the world and everyone in it. But Souls, too, have a history going back thousands of years, and their history keeps coming back.

Some of that history is negative whilst others are positive in their dealings with you. Remember that many of these Souls have a deep hidden agenda from previous existences in another space a different time; this is another subject entirely and very deeply profound. Right now we have to deal with the phenomena of messages.

So, let us play out a possible scenario. You suddenly get a strong message of warning but are unable to explain it logically. It is a feeling of fear and it makes you uncomfortable. Sometimes that feeling could be about another person, someone that you have never met before, but who you just don't like. Never ignore these feelings or push them aside. You are always in dangerous territory when this happens.

The problem is that on the **Default Mode** many people go into denial and ignore feelings of impending disaster. Whenever we ignore those messages, things go wrong or plans go awry. These messages can be early signs of illness in you or others, no future in a given relationship, job or business venture, or the possibility that the person you met isn't a nice person at all.

You will find that life goes around in cycles. Never forget that you are living on a big wheel that is always moving. The wheel slowly reaches the top and if you are not careful, continues on inevitably all of the way down to the bottom again.

A new message can download into your mind but you may prefer to ignore it. Then you find yourself making the mistake of saying or thinking, 'This can never happen again', and boom bang it does happen again.

I remember, a long time ago, a friend said to me, if we took all the weather forecasters and exchanged them for economists, our lifestyle would not change at all, because nobody can really tell you how things are going to turn out.

Life has the habit of taking us by surprise.

Then there are the prophets of doom, who warn you of all sorts of forthcoming disasters. Sometimes they happen and sometimes they don't.

So, what are you going to do when you are in impending disaster mode?

First take yourself way above and try to get a bird's eye view of the situation. Separate yourself from the challenge, try to advise yourself as to how you are going to best handle it. Always keep firmly in your mind that there is a solution out there, as to how to solve it or live with it.

Accepting is important too.

There is another equally important point – a rule dictated by the Sages:

Know and understand a problem in its own good time [(27)]

At first glance it seems to be 'home spun' advice, such as 'Don't cross your bridges before coming to them' and in a way it really is like that, but slightly different.

We must learn to place different challenges into separate boxes. I was once asked 'how do you eat an elephant? If you go straight in and try to consume all of that flesh it just won't work. However, if you take it piece by piece you will eventually consume the whole elephant. That is exactly how you handle challenges, both big and small.

First, make a program of action. Divide your challenges between immediate action items and those that can wait for the future. Then relax and separate yourself... Allow your thoughts to flow... Do not push for an answer. The one you think of immediately, might turn about to be lame. Never act unless the message is clear. Do not be concerned if nothing comes to you straight away. You need to relax and don't allow yourself to be taken over by panic and depression. Don't simply throw up your hands in defeat, or you will have lost before you start.

You will be surprised how the ideas flow at the right time. Sleeping on things is always a healthy approach. Sometimes you have to do the hardest thing. Walk away, handle something else, listen to music, go to a show and remove your mind from the immediate mumbo jumbo that is spinning in your head. Give your brain a chance to sort things out in a logical order. As I said from the beginning, our brain acts like a computer. Give it all the time it needs to store the information, search for similar situations or parallel ones, to dig out potential solutions from its library of previous events and outcomes. You should not be concerned. If you have trained your mind to link on to the Big Brain, then let it Google as much as it wants. Your brain is programmed to feed in the right key words.

I have literally thousands of stories and personal experiences of surprise and satisfaction with problems that sorted themselves out in this way. Many times when I hear myself coming out with an elegant solution or idea, I honestly say aloud,

'I wish that I had thought of that one'.

Knowing and recognising that these solutions and messages are not of your making, understanding that the real source is much bigger than all of us, will strengthen your power to continue to do so. If you don't accept this, you are in danger of being left on your own, back down on the **Default Mode**, because it would seem then that you really do not need any help. Having feelings of pride, cockiness, self-praise and so on actually separates you from this powerful capability.

Remove yourself from the chaos, stay way above it all – That's why you are up here... Ignore everything anybody is telling you, just listen to your messages and act accordingly.

I am going to tell you a very interesting story where I made a decision based on a strong message, which you might call a strong feeling. But what is the difference what you call it, right?

Those strong feelings made me take a decision, which turned out to be the correct choice. The average person who, not understanding what it is to be on the Divine Mode, would never have gone as far as I did. But, when you are on the Divine Mode, and you get a message to stop, walk out or break off from a relationship, don't waste your time; on the other hand, when it tells you to go ahead, go for it.

A long time ago, I had a student in London. She was at the university and one day she said to me, 'I don't know what to do. I'm studying for my doctorate. I have a mentor, a very famous professor. The other day when I went to see him, he had forgotten the subject of my thesis. When he was the one who advised me and now he can't remember?'

She told me that her professor had actually asked, very simply: 'Tell me again what your subject is?'

My immediate answer was, 'Listen to me very carefully. Why do you need another warning, another message? Why don't you go back to your faculty head and tell him you need someone else'.

So she turned around to me and said, 'But this man is very wise'.

Think carefully.
The world is divided...
Between the wise - and the 'otherwise'
Never forget that

Eliyahu Kelman

So, you have to go according to what you call your instinct, your gut feeling and don't ignore the message.

We have a principle – it's a secret in life.

The Final Outcome
is embedded in your first
thoughts and reactions [28]
Turn it over in your mind,
and accept the message
delivered within the first impression
Never talk yourself in, or out,
nor let anyone
persuade you otherwise

Eliyahu Kelman

It does not really matter how logical or illogical that thought is at the time. But, be assured it will happen. So again, the first reaction you have when you meet a person, are given an idea or receive a proposal is the one to go with. If it doesn't seem right, then usually it isn't.

The opposite is also true. If you feel good and comfortable about a person, idea or proposal, then that's the way to go.

So, here is another story to illustrate just that. It happened just before the crash of 2008.

We were working with a great company and lovely people who had developed brilliant software focused on the banking industry. They had found a solution to a major problem that most Banks face as they expand their activities in any specific new venture. The beauty was that it could easily and quickly be adapted to any new product or any other variations of a given theme.

I am not going to go into detail as to what it did, but it was very clever, very advanced, very sophisticated and nothing like the Banks had ever seen before. They had clients, very important clients, well-known Banks, but they needed backing for expansion and to meet the ever-growing demand for their product.

We were called in to help them with the structure and seed capital in preparation for a public issue on the New York Stock Exchange. I believed in everything they were doing, the people, the market and the solutions that they had to offer. So I allocated a team and the necessary funding to enable the project to move forward.

A lot of work and creativity was invested into this project. We teamed up with one of the largest accounting firms in the world in the joint creation of a Business Plan and Offering Memorandum. Our team had worked on this for about a year and we were getting close to the time when we would be able to float on the stock exchange in New York.

We had already lined up the initial investors. Everyone was very excited at the prospects for success. There were so many people who did not want to miss out on this opportunity. We had clients who had been previously successful in backing the right growth company and others who didn't intend to miss their chance this time around, as they had done in the past.

One day, seemingly out of the blue, I suddenly had a gut feeling that something was wrong. I couldn't explain it but the message kept on repeating itself. At night, it kept on coming back and just wouldn't leave me alone. The message clearly said, 'There is going to be a crash'. If that happened, the first thing the Banks would do would be to cut down on this type of expense. They cannot modernise if they have immediate and urgent problems to handle. If our company lost some of their main clients, they would be finished. All of the support would be withdrawn overnight and any flotation would be a dismal failure.

It was a definite warning. And so, what did I do? I called my team together, saying, 'We're not going ahead'. The team was absolutely shocked because we were ready, more than ready, everything lined up for the launch.

Everything had to be put on hold in order to give the company a chance to survive.

'Everyone had gone into denial…
In the real world economists and
financial advisors were
taken completely by surprise
Gale force winds were blowing
from the financial markets,
a catastrophic storm was
about to break, the die was cast,
there was no more doubt,
the crash of 2008 had no chance to abate
For millions of people
there was
no way to bail out'

Eliyahu Kelman

This message was foremost in my mind, disregarding completely the counter arguments that were circulating in the financial world at that time. I told them exactly how we were going to handle this situation, and promised them that they would be thanking me in 6 months' time, when everything would become clear to them.

When expecting a storm
batten down the Hatches

I gave them a detailed plan as to what had to be done.

Take time out, restructure their budget, build their client base, continue development while cutting back on any expansion and unnecessary overheads. This was the time to prepare for a difficult voyage.

I reminded them of a well-known joke, which they would never want to get caught up in. The joke went like this,

'What was the most dangerous business transaction ever?'

When Noah floated an ark…
Just before the whole world
was going into liquidation

'I'm afraid that is exactly what you are going to witness happening'.

The message was clear, I ignored the self-denial of those in the financial community who were declaring in broadcasts, newspaper reports and interviews.

'What are you talking about? Everything is fine. There is plenty of money around. Everybody is investing'.

I was silent because I had the warning and it would not go away.

It wasn't a question of **Abra-Ca-Dabra** so much that time. It was a matter of **Certainty, Absolute Certainty**. I knew, in this particular case, that the message was a correct message out of experience of being on the Divine Mode for a long, long time.

Well, let me tell you what happened… Within less than three weeks, the first Bank folded in the United States. Things started to rock a bit. Central Banks were a bit worried and we received the first sign that the message was right. One of their clients, who fed them with 40% of their revenue, told them that they were shelving the project for the moment. He called me up and asked me, 'How did you know?'

I said, 'Listen, I have been around a long time. One day when we publish the book, I will let you read it and then you will know, but we have no time for that now, you need to concentrate on your company'.

The crash came. He survived the crash, because he had listened to my warning and made the necessary adjustments within his company. I assured him that we would not claim back any of our investment up to then.

'One day when you make money, you will owe it to us'.

He sailed through. He survived on 30% of the clients he had before, but he carried on, determined and with Certainty, Absolute Certainty. I had taught him this and that was how he lived.

As we move forward in this journey, we find that we get deeper and deeper into learning and acquiring the secrets and tools needed to guide us towards dealing with everything and everyone in our lives.

You will learn in the next chapter about the no Accident is an Accident principle and how to handle difficult and tragic situations.

You will learn about remarkable real-life stories dealing with tragedies, but also the good side. You will learn about a major life changing shock that provided the solution for the next biggest shock wave that was coming up just behind. I will teach you how to get rid of negative thoughts and stave off Brain-Pollution. The inner secrets of a great marriage and making other relationships work will be revealed to you. You will be amazed at how simple and easy it really is. Further you will learn about the DNA of the Soul, a communication system to help you conjure up the people you need to meet or see.

There is still so much to learn and I am so happy you will be going with me. So, before we embark on our next amazing journey, take some time now to go into your higher space and **Self-Hypnotise**. Think about all you have learnt in this chapter, apply it to your own life and experiences you have had.

Relax and take it all in. Breathe deeply and take yourself back into outer space.

'Excellence is never an accident.
It is always the result of high intention,
sincere effort and intelligent execution
represents the wise choice of many alternatives.
Choice - not chance, determines your destiny'.

Aristotle

'There are no accidents,
all things have a deep and
calculated purpose.
Sometimes the methods employed
by providence seem strange
and incongruous.
We only have to be patient and
wait for the result.
Then we recognise that no others
would have answered the purpose.
We are rebuked and humbled'.

Mark Twain 1923

Chapter Thirteen

No Accident is an Accident[29]
Life is not always as it seems

- *There is a reason for everything, search for the hidden map and then apply the certainty embedded in the Codes of life*

You have developed and grown so much since we started this voyage together, not only through the meditation, **Abra-Ca-Dabra**, and **Absolute Certainty**, but also in the will, the wish and the desire to open up the channels to receive Real-Time-Streaming messages and information into your brain.

We have a lot of work ahead of us, moving forward whilst going back to the previous chapters again and again, meditating again, absorbing, internalising, and even discussing all that you have learnt with your family and close friends.

If you want to write to me, go to my website and tell me about your experiences and progress, your challenges and ideas. I would love to hear from you.

We have now reached the point where it is time to discuss another type of message.

The story I am going to tell you today is from a personal experience, which will show you that you cannot predict an inevitable outcome. The subject is 'No Accident is an Accident'.

Although we think often that things happen to us in life, seemingly by chance, an unexpected meeting, a big mistake, or a blurting out of something to the wrong person.

Many times I have continued email correspondence on a 'reply to all' basis and then realised I had forgotten to delete one or two recipients, ending up with the wrong people seeing what was meant to be a draft. These can sometimes be outrageous mistakes. In my experience, it always turned out to be a good thing that it happened.

We all are taking a sure path in life,
full of decisions and freedom to choose
Just watch out for the sign posts
along the way
Be certain and sure whatever your choice,
be ever alert for that inner voice
Always remember and keep in your mind,
what is happening in your life
is from the Divine
No Accident is an Accident,
let the story unfold,
taking you forward
towards your pot of gold

Eliyahu Kelman

At first you think, 'What a terrible tragedy. How am I going to get through this?' But, until you realise that the Divine had something up its sleeve and if you had known it from the beginning, you would have looked at life differently. But, you see, up on the Divine Mode, there is no excuse for that. Because you have to have certainty that things are only done with love. However tragic it looks, there is always an explanation.

Now, what we are going to do is to reflect on this story, relax, and think of the other type of message, a straightforward message, a message received from another party…

You suddenly receive terrible news. Something happened and you think, 'This is the end of my life' or 'I do not know what to do. This is such a change. I don't know whether I can take it or not'.

You need to have that certainty in your mind that it is for the good and that you have got to go seek…

The silver lining in the cloud

It is a lovely expression, really on the Divine Mode, though the majority of people simply do not understand its inner meaning.

But, first, let me tell you a story about a friend of mine that I knew in London, she came to my courses and was excited about them.

One day she told me her story.

'You are so right. Tragedy can turn out to be good. I was in Nazi Germany, but living in a small village far from the city, so far nobody had touched us. We thought we were safe and my father would travel regularly to England on business.

The war with Britain had not started yet, and the Nazis were well entrenched in Europe.

One day we received a telegram, in those days that was how you communicated, Faxes, email or phone were just not on the scene or even a figment of imagination. Those were the days when it cost more than $5 a minute for an international call, speaking on a phone that went through a local switchboard'.

She took a breath and continued, 'My mother received a telegram telling her that my father had been badly injured in a car accident.

The telegram read, 'You had better come with the family immediately to be with him, just in case he does not survive'. Of course my mother was very upset and heartbroken. She had to quickly gather enough money together for tickets and expenses in London.

We headed for the airport and got on the first plane flying to London'.

My friend was quite emotional by this stage, and so was I, but she carried on, 'Well, let me tell you. Whilst we were boarding the plane, the Nazis marched into our village and rounded up every Jewish person living there. We were, of course, on the plane, not knowing what was going on back home. That was the tragedy that saved our family's lives. I know first-hand that you are right! But when it happened, for us, it was a tragedy and it was sad that it had to happen just in order to save our lives.

My only regret is that no similar tragedy or miracle saved so many of our friends and relatives from being murdered by the Nazi's'.

The subject of why something happens to one person or a set of people, and not another, is an entirely different angle, a much, much higher and at the same time, a deeper level of the soul. We will be working on this question together.

It took a long time for her father to recover but he had some money put away in London, they were all saved and able to rebuild their lives. For me, that was a beautiful story of how the Divine works in mysterious ways.

Now, I want to get on with another amazing story that happened to another very, very close friend of mine.

He was a Sales Manager in a very large company and had been working there for over 20 years.

The company ran into difficulties, so they made a list of people that they felt could be sent into early retirement. They offered them all very generous severance payments to take early retirement.

To his surprise, even though he was so valuable and key to the company's success,

The CEO had called him in for a chat.

'You know, we like you very much, but this was a decision that we had to take, so these are our terms and conditions for severance and early retirement'.

'A younger man will cost us less', and 'We have all the clients that you have been paid for and accumulated over the years. We have considered this very carefully and much to my personal regret you are on the list'.

He was shattered and broken-hearted because he enjoyed his job. He liked working there and liaising with his sales team. He liked attending the annual parties.

He came to me late that night and sat down, almost in tears. He was most definitely broken-hearted. He related everything that I told you and that's how he felt – deep, deep inside.

'What am I going to do now? I can't stop working. But on the other hand, where will I go? How can I start over now? There are younger people who are moving in; anyway, most of the companies out there have their Sales Managers already. All of them are both well-established and entrenched'.

So, I turned around to him and I said, 'Listen my friend, you know I love you very much. Have you thought that there was a reason for this…? The Manager and owners of the company are, after all, only agents and messengers? And if they are insisting like this, then it is most probably the best and most logical move for the company to make.

The very key and heart of their business is sales. Without sales, they will carry on sailing down the river without a rudder. They are clearly finished, and are letting you go.

There must be another reason, because G-d loves you. And, while you don't know what that reason is right now, you have to believe that this is for the best.

He wouldn't accept it. He was quite upset with me and actually wanted to bop me one.

I let him calm down and continued.

'I suggest you call up the CEO in the morning and just say, 'Look here, I am not really ready to retire. For me, it is earth shattering. It is very difficult, but the chance of my finding another position at my age and in today's economic environment is going to be literally impossible'.

Tell them that you have to put your kids through university and that you have all sorts of dreams you wanted to accomplish. You need to make them see that the package, while generous, is not enough to cover that, and secure you into the future.

Ask them to come back with another offer. Don't push them and don't suggest how much. Just tell them that you will sign whatever they offer'.

The man wanted to eat me alive! He was livid as hell as he listened to me.

'Getting angry is one thing, but taking my advice is another. If you go in there with confidence and using **Abra-Ca-Dabra**, you will see they will give you another offer. If you just sit back and accept what they are offering, then you have lost already'.

He was angry with me because I was telling it to him like it was and while he knew I was giving him good advice, he was wallowing in his own self-pity and struggling to see beyond that.

But, nevertheless, he pulled himself out of his doldrums and went to see the CEO the next day. He told him exactly what I had told him to say.

'Look, I am not going to put up any more argument. I understand that you haven't made this decision against me. You have taken this decision, right or wrong, because you think that's the smartest thing to do. But this is what I need and now I will leave it up to you'.

To his great surprise, they added 25% to his severance package, a very generous bonus straight away. He signed and went home a much happier man. But he knew he had to find something to do and quickly.

We all know that when somebody retires and was always a very active person, if he doesn't find something to do, to occupy his day and his mind, he can go downhill very quickly.

My friend left happy but not satisfied, and three weeks later had a massive heart attack. We all rushed to the hospital, totally shocked, as was he. But it was a time when the hospitals didn't have the facilities we have today, now you can go in, they insert a stent and you are right as rain in no time.

Back then, he was living in a time when, if you survived a heart attack, especially a massive heart attack, you were normally confined to a wheelchair and left with a severely limited outlook on life.

'If you think about disaster,
you will get it.
If you brood about death you will
hasten your demise.
Think positively and masterfully,
with confidence and faith.
Life becomes more sure
and fraught with action,
richer in achievement
and experience'.

Swami Vivakananda (1863 - 1902)

I waited for the right opportunity and asked him what he thought about the double tragedy of losing his job and having that heart attack?

Do you remember what I said to you? You thought it was a tragedy but I told you there was something good built in there'.

He said in frustration, 'How can a heart attack be good?'

'My dear friend, on the **Default Mode**, you can't expect nature to change. I told you so many times. The soul goes on forever but the body must wear out, some people earlier and some people later in life'.

I took his hand and continued, 'It isn't a change of life. I assure you, on the Divine Mode, they knew you were going to have this massive heart attack. The biggest blessing was the strong message I downloaded just at the right time. I had no other message to give you, because nothing else would come into my mind at that time. When I gave it to you, I myself, heard it for the first time, can you just imagine what would have happened if they had not made that decision to send you into early retirement? You know as well as I do that there terms would have fallen far short of your plans and dreams'.

He looked at me with absolute wonder.

'Now, you don't have to worry because financially you are sorted out. You can't work, anyway. You are entitled to everything that you are going to get and you are free. So, I suggest you remember who you have to thank, believe that messages should always be listened to, and never be ignored. Always remember that however bad it seems:

'The big boss knows what is good for you'.

This is the meditation that has taken you right throughout this series. Absorb it. Retain it. Internalize it. Go over it again and again. If you have a similar experience, make sure that you listen to the message and with patience, you will learn what it is all about.

Have a short story?
Write to me...
Tell me all about similar
experiences and messages
that you downloaded
or missed and left you confused.
I would love to hear from you
as I want to get that good feeling
from your wonderful stories,
just like you have experienced
through mine
eliyahu@metoo-youtoo.net

No Accident is an Accident
it's part of your life
Just like magic,
the unexpected appears
Just like magic,
turning everything around
Expect the unexpected,
where surprises abound,
waiting for you around the corner,
where success can be found

Eliyahu Kelman

Negativity,
a force we all must fight,
without darkness there can be no light
Chaos on the Default Mode reigns supreme
Brain-Pollution and confusion
is all that is seen

Break free, break free...
From a life run on the Default,
soar up to the Divine,
a sure life of Certainty,
forever we shine

Eliyahu Kelman

Chapter Fourteen

Staving off Brain Pollution

- *Applying the Inner Secrets to actively eliminate Negative Thought*

- *Make events turn out for the good, however bad they may seem*

I want you to switch gears. We have been following a path up until now, helping you to learn how to relate to everything that you are doing in your personal life. But now we need to take it even further.

Do you remember right at the beginning when you saw the clip that introduced you to the website and to this book?

'Wouldn't it be a dream if everybody came with a Handbook, if everybody came into this world with a step-by-step guide? How to handle your spouse or partner, work with your children, with your workmates or your classmates, or at university, your friends and even the people that surround you. The events and the challenges you have to face every day'.

Well, here we are! Many of the people who are reading this have already enjoyed special relationships for years, some are doing well, and some are challenged. In many cases if it is going well, nobody knows why or how. And if it is not going so well, you don't even know how you got in that space. That is what I want to talk about today.

It is important to remember that we are all on the first level, still working on building those steps to reach the first floor of our beautiful villa way out in the countryside, immersed in the sounds of birdsong, flowing water and peace, all surrounded by beautiful scenery. It has to be like that because this is the life that you want to live.

Of course, realities are realities, if you suffer from Brain-Pollution, and you have difficulties and challenges, then we have to deal with them as well.

We all have a big problem in life. Let's identify this force as a man called Murphy.

We all know Murphy, better known as 'Murphy's Law'. You can't see Murphy. You can only sense him when he is around. This man, this hidden force wanders around the world causing chaos to all and sundry. He especially seeks out those who are enjoying peace, quiet, harmony and tranquillity. We often wonder how the peace and quiet is suddenly shattered by an unexpected controversy, a word in the wrong place at the wrong time or an accident that upsets everything. When things are running smoothly, suddenly everything goes off track.

This is a phenomenon that we learn to live with. Murphy is in our mind continuously, whispering nonsense into our ear and our minds. The problem is, each and every one of us have that alien inside wherever we go and whatever we do. This alien is always ready to pounce, armed with arrows of negativity, depression, laziness and controversy.

Actually, he is called, by some, 'The Evil Inclination', but I don't want to name this inner negative force 'The Evil Inclination'. I rather like the word 'Murphy'. Why? Because I can identify with him, an all-embracing force who must be treated as the enemy.

Just like we have to do with messages, our radar must be up all the time, watching out for his presence in our decision-making process, thoughts and mind.

Can you imagine this? You are lying in bed early in the morning; you know that you have to get going? But it's Sunday! So maybe you can lie in just a little bit longer, thinking to yourself, 'Well, what does it matter? The children will wait. My wife will wait. I won't do all the activities that I intended to do today'.

There is work to do in the garden, there are things to prepare, things to write and all sorts of extra tasks to attend to. Then your mind wanders to other seemingly random thoughts. You analyse what people really mean to you. All sorts of negative thoughts come clamouring into your mind. Then you find yourself fighting back with your own arguments, getting weaker and weaker. You doze off once again.

And that is 'Murphy', taking the centre stage in your life. You have to say to yourself,

'Wait a minute! Murphy got up before me. I am going to get out of bed now. Why should I have him wandering around and already working on me? I am not going to allow it!'

Whenever I walk down the street or I come across the 'Murphy' in my mind, I shout out in Arabic (I have no idea why my mind chooses that language) roukh min hon! Get out of here! I don't want to see you!' And then I laugh to myself.

Because if you recognise that all negative thoughts, all arguments, all controversy, comes from 'Murphy', you will know why? He wants to make chaos in this world. All chaos comes from there, because if everybody recognises each other's rights and they remember their own obligations, then there isn't chaos. Just be aware that chaos is around, waiting to pounce at any given moment.

Why is 'Murphy' so interested in this chaos? You now want to pull yourself up onto the Divine Mode, and that comes with a lot of changes and challenges. At the same time, you want to maintain a good relationship with your wife.

Well 'Murphy' is not happy if you have a happy marriage or you get on with your kids. He is much happier if you fight and then say to yourself, 'I am going to look for better pastures'. He lets hell loose into your life, whether it is in your family, your business or your finances. That is, if you give him any small chance to come in to your life. A crack in your armour of defences can grow gradually into a big split.

Why? Because, when you say, 'What do I need it for?' He wants you to continue with, 'I will go and have an affair. I will find another girlfriend. I want to get out of this marriage'.'

I am going to ignore my children, get angry with them and not talk to them'. Yet, you are supposed to love them. You can be angry with what they do, but not with them as individuals.

One of the most powerful tools that he uses is your perception of truth and honesty, right and wrong or black and white. Suddenly you find yourself developing an answer, an excuse for granting yourself permission and a licence to do whatever you like to do, regardless. We call it the 'dark grey shadow between the two possibilities'. After all it is not so bad or wrong. Who will know anyway?

Everyone does it. Why shouldn't I take what I am really entitled to? He stole it anyway, so finders keepers.

There are so many different levels of truth to choose from, thinking that way can 'hold you back' from climbing up and onto the Divine Mode. There is a price to pay for absolutely everything that we do. There is one price for what we do, and one for what we don't do.

So you might say, 'Why was that challenge put into this world...? Why does the Soul have to suffer...?'

To answer: Fighting it makes you stronger. That is the whole point of the challenges we face in life.

There is that old adage, 'What doesn't kill you, makes you stronger'. Keep moving forward, developing your Soul and safeguarding it. You can turn negatives into positives. When I was a young man everybody loved the saying:

Well, it does not mean much to us today, but what's behind it all? When you are pressured, under great strain, or in a hole, don't keep digging..., make the most of it and rescue what you can from that situation. Simple misunderstanding and overreaction is caused by not thinking things through.

There is a famous line that George Burns used when quoting Julius Caesar, 'Let all of the poison in the lake hatch out'.

It is remarkable how different things turn out to be when you take a closer look at the situation, or in the behaviour of others. Do we really know what drives another person in their decision making process? Perhaps it was the result of misunderstanding and not reading the road map properly.

Understanding people and how they think is vital to developing solid relationships. And the key is taking the time to listen to them, really listen.

Take a moment now to think and meditate about when Murphy sat on your shoulder and spewed negative thoughts into your head. How did you react? Did you go with the flow? Or did you stubbornly tell him to go away? Right now, it doesn't matter what you did. It matters that you acknowledge that you are only human and will falter from time to time. But know that you can make the choice.

Take situations when you falter
and turn them towards the positive.
Imagine yourself doing the opposite
of what you are doing right now.

What do you think
the result would have been?

Let's not be complacent,
whatever we do
Never be satisfied,
see life through
When challenges, tragedies,
come into our lives
It's there to strengthen us,
train us, make us immune
Moving up to the next stage,
with our lives well tuned,
climbing ever higher,
on our ladder of destiny
Developing our purpose,
our potential with intensity

Eliyahu Kelman

The soul connection
goes way back in time,
as Soulmates on the level Divine
Each family member is linked,
one to the other
A bond so strong never to be severed
from generation to generation,
the story goes on
A deep spiritual bonding, a responsibility
and feeling too deep to describe
When souls get together relationships thrive
The hidden secrets and rules act as a guide,
Making relationships so special
they forever abide

Eliyahu Kelman

Chapter Fifteen

The Handbook for Life

- *Harnessing mental telepathy*

- *Everybody has a hidden power to actually conjure up the people and solutions needed right now*

These Handbooks are really all about direct relationships between Souls. Once we learn to tap into each other's Soul we get to the very core of the Operating System. So before moving on we need to understand a bit more about the inter relationship between Souls.

Family is the key for making up the Soul, as that is where the roots of the Soul lie. Imagine that each Soul is like a tree with many twigs and branches, going back many generations and thousands of years.

That is why the Soul relates so closely with family members all over the world. This goes even further than just one tree. What we are talking about is a whole forest of trees. When you consider that families intermarry with the relatives you have, so when we meet someone we are related to, through that forest way back in time, we can find that special feeling, of finding a Soulmate, a shared history.

On the other hand, there are family trees that have a history of enmity and even revenge in their psyche. That is why, sometimes, when we meet a complete stranger, we get a very uncomfortable feeling in their company. The Sages advise us to move away and not continue any form of relationship with those people.

Your Soul transmigrates but this subject is deep and needs to be studied when you are well established on the Divine Mode level. We will get there eventually. This is just a small insight into how to interrelate, why people do what they do. A lot can be learned from the special Handbook for your Spouse. A lot of surprises, but that is what is embedded in each and every Handbook for handling other people in your lives.

It is all about the messages that are being transferred continuously between Souls, consciously or through our sub-conscious. Isn't it interesting that you can walk in to a room, look at somebody, and immediately strike up a warm relationship.

You can walk into a shop, as I once did with my wife, and have strong negative feelings to the point of being frightened of the woman who owned the shop.

My wife was looking at some dresses that interested her and she couldn't understand why I suddenly came over and pulled out of the shop as fast as I could. I was receiving the vibes from the shopkeepers Soul. How does that happen? Way back in time there was a hatred embedded in this women's soul and I was receiving the vibes.

Because the Soul has migrated from generation to generation and we all have roots. We come from different branches and you have to imagine that the Soul is like a part of a tree. You have the trunk, which is the main anchor, and then you have the branches and the twigs, which are made up of your ever-growing family.

Why is that? It is because your Soul is communicating through your body, and the Soul has a memory. Your body doesn't always know and usually cannot know the story behind it, but I would like to illustrate that a little bit later on.

So, we have this enormous tree with lots and lots of branches, so many we can't even count them. In fact, the number turns itself into a forest because each single twig falls down with its seed and starts another family, and another family, and then another, forever expanding. There are some families I know, where the great-grandparents have something approaching 200 living descendants within their lifetime.

What about the people you love? We have a great expression in English, 'Well, she's my Soulmate', or 'My friend, a wonderful Soul'. We use that expression to show that we have a special care for that person, a deeper connection, but that person could be from the other side of the world. I met my wife in Singapore and she came from Iraq. I came all the way from England via France.

G-d obviously uses computers to match up from those great distances. The main thing is that it works, and is still working. What helps a lot is that I follow the rules in the Handbook I wrote.

People migrate, just as Souls migrate. People move around the world; change their jobs, their home. These changes are sometimes forced, sometimes voluntarily, as when marrying into other families. It's quite remarkable that none of us know where these roots will lead to, we do get surprises... One day, you could meet somebody and feel good about them. They may have a different colour, a different religion, but you consider them a Soulmate. If you feel a connection, never ignore it.

- Get close to those you feel comfortable with.

- Run a mile from the ones where you get that bad feeling...

However slight that feeling... Don't trust them! Don't become friends with them and don't do business with them. Not trusting them will solve half your problems before you start.

There is another important rule within that. I give it to you in three very important words

KISO - means 'His pocket'

and

KOSO - means 'His cup when he is drunk',

and

KAASO - means his anger

KISO, KOSO, KAASO [30]

These words are Hebrew. It is worthwhile trying to remember those words, because we have no equivalent in any other language that automatically reveals the inner working of a person's real personality. Leo Roston, an American humorist, very aptly named these three - Koso, Kiso and Kaaso as 'his tipping' – 'his tippling' and 'his temper'. One can very accurately gauge another person's personality or character by these three words, how they react when they are drunk, how they deal with money and how they behave when angry.

KISO

When it comes to Kiso, his pocket, we can ask questions: 'Is he generous? Is he tight? Has he got his hand in your pocket or in his own?' You know whom you are dealing with by the way he handles the subject of money.

KOSO

Koso for when he is drunk. When a person is inebriated they will let their guard down and behave as their true character depicts. They will say all sorts of things that are in their heart and while others may defend them by saying 'Well, he was not insulting us… He was drunk and did not mean what he said'. No! Drunkenness unlocks the secrets of a man's heart, reveals what he is truly thinking inside.

His statements could very well be the truth. His statements could be completely unfounded, but if that person reveals that they hate you, want to kill you or steal from you, or in fact want to do anything that is bad and dangerous, run away. Walk out of their life.

KAASO

There are many people who use anger to control and frighten their family, or people they deal with in everyday life. The victims defence mechanism is normally to shy away, in order not to trigger off another outburst from the angry party. Most people will give in to the demands put forward by a 'temper box'. They generally are too afraid to tackle the issue at hand, the issue being the angry person. But they do know what their true personality is, from observing their behaviour when angry.

Kaaso, interestingly enough, is seen as one of the most dangerous of the deadly sins, and on the flipside, patience is seen as the antidote. Patience allows the afflicted person to take time to think about their reaction and calm themselves down.

That should always be our response if we do not want to live a lie or a life of abuse. When someone reveals their real self, then that is how you must react. Otherwise you will live permanently on the Default Mode.

Perhaps this is the most important chapter, in learning how to live with other people and if they generate positive vibes accept them as they are.

I would like to remind you what I said when I wrote about people living in a spacesuit? Because you are sitting there, in control of the spacesuit in your brain, your eyes see 180 degrees, even the whole horizon! But, when you look at someone else, you see that person as limited within their own body. You cannot imagine that they are taking up more space in that spacesuit. This also creates problems. But you must try all the time to remember, that when you are dealing with other people, they also view the world at 180 degrees. They also have special feelings. They too want to be convinced that you are a possible Soulmate.

You might ask, 'Do I really need to be a Soulmate with my boss?' Simple answer ... Yes, you do, or your business relationship just does not work. You will be clashing all of the time. Mutual trust comes from Soul relationships.

People have the tendency to damage themselves and to damage each other in the process. With this Soul relationship, we soon realise that it goes very much deeper than that. The more you look out for these experiences the more you actually see the relationship growing.

I want to link this together with what we learnt about messages.

We get messages from people and Downloading Messages into our minds. Many times, the messages are from somebody who became very close to you because you are Soulmates. And many, many times it is from people you haven't seen for years. Develop this sense to the Nth degree and you too will be able to communicate through mental telepathy[31] and actually conjure them up. This is very advanced into the Divine Mode but in time you can enjoy these experiences as well.

I want to share with you a few incidences that happened to me and also to a friend of mine, just to illustrate the effect of the Soul being attached one to the other.

I was working on a major project in Switzerland and had travelled up into the mountains to stay in a beautiful hotel resort, there to do my work. Sometimes you need a good environment to meditate and think.

One day, whilst sitting at the breakfast table, the sun streaming into the dining room, I was admiring the stunning view through the windows. Snow-capped mountains and loads of people skiing, it was wonderful.

I sat there thinking, 'There is a particular legal specialist that I need to see, as soon as possible, in order to carry on developing and completing my latest project. There is only one man I really need to see, a smart lawyer, a lecturer and professor - a world expert in this particular field, also a very close friend.

I thought to myself, 'Well, I'm up here in the mountains, how wonderful it would be if he was here right now… It would be great taking a walk in the mountains and discussing this project, with the benefit of his full and undivided attention'.

It was such a strong feeling of connection between our Souls that I knew that something very deep was happening, that I was getting a message. I looked up and I saw somebody walk into the restaurant in casual clothes.

Whom did I see? None other than that self-same lawyer friend I hadn't seen for three or four years. As I saw him sit down it was surreal, watching the scenario that had just played out in my mind actually taking place in front of me; my brain went into overdrive and I went over and gave him a big hug, delighted to see him. Flabbergasted, he reacted enthusiastically.

'You know, I had just conjured you up in my mind, and you walked in! I actually arranged for you to get here… Tell me what are you doing here…?'

'Well I'll tell you the truth; I am not quite sure how it happened, because it certainly was not planned that way. I have no idea why I am here either'.

I sensed my enthusiasm rising… 'I will tell you why, but first tell me your story. How did you get here?'

'What happened was, I was booked for a series of lectures at the university in Zurich. My secretary had arranged my flights to take me straight from here to Holland to give some lectures in Amsterdam and to lead an important focus group. The flights were booked and I was ready to fly direct.

I have no idea what made me double check my schedule of lectures but I found that my secretary had made a mistake. There were one-and-a-half days in between and I did not need to fly to Holland straight away'.

My friend continued, 'I thought to myself 'How nice it would be to take some time off, go to the mountains and take a break at this hotel. My intention was to spend the time walking in the mountains, thinking and reflecting'.

'My dear friend that is exactly what I was thinking of a little while ago'. And I told him what happened with me, my thoughts and reveries.

We were completely overwhelmed and realised of course that:

No Accident
is an
Accident

I told him that by sheer mental force I had conjured him up. A back message was sent to him. He had picked it up and headed for this hotel.

In Switzerland you have many choices, so the fact that he had chosen that hotel, was a miracle, or was it?

We did spend that day walking in the mountains. It was absolutely incredible! We became even closer, as we mapped out the legal solution that was needed for this major international project of mine. After that we each went our own way and carried on as we were before - Mission accomplished!

This experience speaks for itself. Many, many times in my life, I have made up my mind and believed that:

Even
the seeming Impossible
can become Possible

Always with **Certainty, Absolute Certainty**, make up your mind that the Impossible is actually going to happen. This is how we can solve problems, you simply say to yourself:

'I need this type of person in my life'.

When you are determined and certain, that person will actually turn up. I have many more fantastical stories to tell you about this magical phenomenon.

How does it happen? First there must be a Soul connection, not necessarily with people you already know. What is very important for this to work, is that there always has to be a Soul connection. You never know how far the connection goes back, but you can depend on it, with the right determination, it will appear suddenly and unexpectedly so.

The way to see whether there is a Soul connection works like this:

First of all, let the other person talk, allow them to tell you what they need, what their worries and their problems are. Let them speak; don't just go straight into what you want to tell them. They will feel whether there is a Soul connection or not. And when you make that Soul connection, you may find that for that first meeting you won't even talk about the subject you came together to discuss. Why? To find their own balance they need help and sympathy. They needed understanding and somebody to talk to. Most people do. Most people are very lonely.

Generally, people speak at each other rather than to each other. Even friends are busy telling their own stories to each other and just waiting for the other one to finish so they can get on with theirs. That is not the way one should conduct relationships and it certainly won't bring you any closer.

The computer language, I spoke of before, helps us to understand this better. Always let the other person download first what they have in their mind. They have a need to tell you. People are very much like computers. First a programmer programs a computer, creating a base, a program in which to upload information. We all know full well that a computer cannot work simultaneously both ways. You first upload, and then you can compute and download. Whilst the computer is computing or refreshing, you have to wait, or do something else. You can't key anything in whilst this is happening.

Well, the same principle applies exactly with a human being. You sometimes get them at the wrong moment, for what you want to discuss or do. How many times, in the interlude to an intimate moment, will the scenario often go like this: -The wife or girlfriend will turn around and say, 'I have a headache'. She doesn't have a headache. It is just the wrong moment for her. She feels under pressure. She needs to talk. So, let her talk. It could even be the other way round, although most men don't use the 'headache' excuse.

Understand you're not being rejected. Understand that people are not turning you away. Even remember this when you are selling something and they say no. So, why did they allow you to sit and talk about it in the first place? The answer really is yes but what they are really saying is, 'You have to convince me'. And that is how it is with relationships as well.

Now, we are ready to meditate on everything that we have learnt today.

It might be a good idea to do the **Stand-Up** Meditation in order to get you in the mood,

Then sit down relax and meditate.

Try to think about what your relationships are like with the different people in your life. Who do you think you should terminate and with whom should you continue? Which relationships should you change and try harder with. Remember it is not only about you. Work on it.

Listen to other people, because they are a Soul like you. They have the same needs, fears and desires as you do. Decide to work on it. Nothing is done without working on it. It is the old-fashioned way. Work on your friendships. Work on helping other people.

In fact, if you just think outwardly, looking for ways of how you can help others all the time; you will find that you will build strong relationships quicker. Think to yourself, 'How can I make them happy? How can I satisfy them?' Their reaction will be to bend over backwards to do the same for you. It is like living a mirrored life. Whatever you do, will come in return. For whatever you don't do the outcome will be obvious. Think of all the people you deal with in your life and how one by one you will gradually change their lives and yours.

It's all about me, it's all about you…
soulmates together side-by-side,
choosing a partner is a challenge in life,
be it a friend, a husband or even a wife
Remember the rule that will act as your guide,
when you bond with her mother
your choice is quite clear
You have found your Soulmate
and the time is now ripe
Just like her mother, her brother,
you are all the same type
Nurture the friendship, keep it going forever,
with complete understanding and caring
Make her your princess for life,
that was her dream and you are her prince
Watch out for Murphy the purveyor of strife,
listen out for messages and hold firm
to your partner in life

Eliyahu Kelman

Chapter Sixteen

A Handbook for Partners in Life

...Conflict Resolution

- *The Codes of Life teach us how to safeguard our marriage and lifetime partnerships*

- *Keeping the feeling of romance alive, always fresh and refreshed*

- *Handling potential conflicts, even those that can't be avoided*

So, now we will give our attention to the Handbook for your Partner in Life.

A story told about Margaret Thatcher, a real tough lady. Her husband goes into a book store and asks, 'Have you got a book with which I can learn how to control my wife?'

'Sir, you will find fiction upstairs'.

We all know that it isn't really fiction, when we understand it a little bit more. The joke is trying to tell us that Margaret was as complex as a fiction novel. Now what you need to know is how to treat your wife or girlfriend like a princess. In fact, all of the females in your life must be treated in the same way, 24/7, like a princess.

It can prove to be quite a challenge, especially if you don't see it that way. Most people can't see why it's necessary.

Let us give this some serious thought. When she was a little girl, she was her father and grandparent's princess. She loved to dress up, all the time, in beautiful clothes. She felt like a princess and she dreamt of being a princess one day. That is why little girls love the story of Cinderella, a prince coming to rescue them, and all other similar stories. They are the favourites for little girls and even bigger girls.

Bigger girls dream, also, of being a princess. Think about it. Why is it when we get married the bride is actually dressed like a princess? Because that is the life you are really promising her. When you courted her, you treated her like a princess. You bought her chocolates, some flowers and gave her respect, opened the car door for her and lent her your jacket when she was cold.

You really worked very hard to create a good impression and make her happy. Of course, you were probably head over heels in love and she responded, reciprocating in exactly the same way. So, as long as you kept up the role of prince and princess, she really felt like one.

Everything in life has a trade off, and providing the couple can keep up this 'play acting' the marriage will really survive as a 'fairy tale love story'.

Here you are, on your wedding day, getting married to this beautiful princess. In fact, the bridal dresses worn today make a bride look even better than in real life.

Now, you are called the 'Groom'. Have you ever thought of that? You're actually dressed like a lackey, very smart with a tie, and you have to serve your princess. You know what the word 'Groom' means? …it used to be one of the lowest grades of employee working at a stately home, a man who looked after the horses. His duties were to groom and saddle horses, and drive them when the princess was in the carriage, because that is what he was hired to do.

Well of course, it cannot just be one-sided, because what you have to do is to say, 'Look, you are my number one and I am number two in this marriage'. I promise you that your wife will be extremely worried and surprised when you start acting on it.

When she shouts at you and says, 'You are a workaholic!' you should use your wife's name and say, 'No, I am an Alice-aholic' (substitute your partner's name here!), because, that's how it has to be. The trade-off is great. What happens in return is that your wife will still feel that you are her prince.

She will still feel that you can and do treat her with respect; and in return she will treat you with respect. She will reciprocate with more love than you can ever dream of or think of, and she will treat you as her prince.

So, what's the problem? When you stop, when you get fed up, when you get tired, when you get stuck in front of a television or a card game, or are off drinking with your friends – then what happens? She starts to think that perhaps you have found another princess.

She starts reacting to her insecurity and the atmosphere changes.

The problem is that for every action there is a reaction. Instead of examining your inner thoughts and actions you react and 'blow it'.

Another important fact to remember is that when a woman gets angry and you ask her directly what the real reason is for her anger or impatience, she really does not have the answer. Women have powerful senses and feelings. Unlike a man, she reacts with emotion, because that is what it is all about.

What is behind this? What can be the cause? It is simpler than you think. A woman's radar is always up, listening out for messages. She has a remarkable sense for what is going on. How many times have you have come home in a good mood, perhaps brought her a little gift, or have good news to share with her. You walk in and you see a sour face, for no apparent reason or so you think. You are tired; perhaps you had a hard and frustrating day at work and you don't need this, so you react immediately and then all hell breaks loose. You actually lose control of the situation.

Dr Eric Berne, the creator of the concept of 'transactional analysis' tells us about the theory that he developed as a result of an extensive research into relationships. The title that took him to fame… 'The Games People Play'.

The first thing that must be remembered is that people cannot fight alone; they always need a sparring partner.

After all how long can you shout for, if no one responds?

The advice he gives is; just say to yourself, 'I am not joining in this game'. Very hard, but if you are tough with yourself it works. Go deaf and wait till the waters have subsided.

Now back to the Sages who advise us as to how we should handle this type of situation. Always remember that your friend, your partner, your wife or girlfriend will be hurting. They sense that something is going on but they can't quite put their finger on it. So they start making random accusations, complaints present or historic, whether or not anything actually happened. Never answer. That is just too dangerous. It just serves to fan the flames. Wait patiently and quietly say, 'Come, let's search together as to what it is I did during the day that is bringing you all of these messages'.

You and your wife must remember that she is a 'Boom Box', where everything gets broadcast through her. That's right. She has this uncanny sixth sense. Be honest with yourself and her. Did you do something disloyal, like flirting with someone whether innocently or not? Did you go out for lunch or a coffee with one of your female colleagues or a client? What innocent thoughts (or not so innocent) went through your mind at that time? Were you unfair or dishonest in any situation during the day? Is there something going on that you wouldn't like your wife to know about? There can be a myriad of happenstances that will trigger this reaction off in her.

Your partner wants to protect her little nest from all outsiders and anyone or anything that will take your attention away from her. If you are away all day and sometimes work through the night, this is not exactly a princess's dream of how her life would turn out with her prince. Understanding each other's feelings and emotions is extremely important. What do you do in order to take back a smidgen of control over this potential threat to the harmony that you so much need in your life?

It is simple really. Just let her know that she is the centre of your life in so many small ways without affecting your routine or outside obligations. Keep calling her in the middle of the day, ask her how she is feeling, tell her that you keep thinking of her and can't get her out of your mind. You were doing this during your courting days, so just keep courting.

Do whatever you did to hold her in your life, when you were trying to draw her permanently into your life. Show her that you are cancelling meetings just for her. Have that drink with her at the end of the day instead of with your friends and colleagues. Find any excuse to have her participate in your life during the day. Instead of arranging a business lunch with someone else, arrange one with her. Do you remember in the beginning, that is exactly what you did?

You always found a way to reschedule. She knew that it was important to you. Make sure that THIS feeling does not fade with time.

Don't get caught up in Murphy's whirlwind.

Bitterness and anger will drive you out, you will try to seek peace elsewhere and you will search for another princess. That is exactly what your princess is trying to avoid.

Ask yourself sincerely, 'How and why did I choose her in the first place?' During the time that you were courting and everybody was dressing up and playing their role perfectly. That's how you both felt and you were sincere about it. So, don't stop, keep it up and you will make your relationships even deeper.

How do you test that you are committing to the right princess? I will tell you how.

We go back to the ancient Sages, who gave us a lot of sound advice. The first rule is to hold firm to your partner and her family, it shouldn't be the other way around.

So it is important to research how your marriage and relationships will develop.

If you get on well and you think alike, then you'll realise where she, is coming from. Get to know your mother-in-law. You will, essentially, be meeting your wife and how she will behave in the future.

Right now, the young lady is playing out her role; she might even be telling you all sorts of stories about how her family are treating her.

It is important to remember that most people in time revert back to type.

What all this is teaching you is that eventually this will be the woman you will be living with. And you have to decide if that is really what you want? Sometimes it is very difficult because you are madly in love with her. On the other hand, that doesn't stay forever. That is what you will have to reconsider. However, it does not necessarily mean that if you don't like the mother-in-law or her brother, that you should walk away.

Remember, people who come from the same background generally act alike. You, too, will also revert back to type, the type you know, the type you like. If your mother behaves in the same way as her mother does, and your brother likewise, then you would probably make an ideal couple, because that is what you are used to in your own lives. You are already used to that background music because you grew up with it.

All Souls are equal, whatever the gender, so make sure that you have found a real Soulmate. Right now she is the other half, but just remember, when you are married you become one Soul, seamless and together. Marriages are made in heaven before your Souls came down and entered your human bodies. If she is a Soul in a woman's body, this means that she is superior and her job is to help you, and you as the man have to work on yourself 24/7.

It is for you to strive to live on the Divine Mode, as she is already inclined that way. That is what the One-Soul, the Soulmate concept is all about. You can always tell if you might have made the wrong choice; if she opposes your new way of life and does not want to participate. Her role is to help you to get there and she should naturally feel good about it – Full stop!

On the Divine Mode she gets messages, but does not always understand. Let me tell you how I've dealt with this challenge ever since the early years of our marriage.

I sit my wife down and say, 'Look, let's relax. Let us search today what I did or what I might have done to be causing this unrest within you'. She does not know what is happening but she is giving you a message, you know what? Every single time you will find an answer, my advice is don't go to bed until you are both happy, even if you've got to keep her up until 2:00 or 3:00 in the morning. My wife used to doze off… I would bring her coffee after coffee to keep her awake so we could finish.

I would say, 'No! We aren't going to bed with this atmosphere, nor are we going to get stubborn or negative towards each other, we must try to sort this one out together and understand why you are under such pressure - then we can go to bed'.

Of course there is much, much more to discuss in the Handbook for Partners in Life.

If you follow the Codes of Life embedded in the ancient writings of the Sages, which go back even to the Book of Creation written by Abraham. You will see the theme picked up again and again throughout the ages.

There is harmony in creation and in every living thing, including the seas, the planets, the stars, the vast distances of interstellar space, as well as the inner space of our minds.

Meditate on all of all that you have learnt today. Look yourself straight in your mind's eye and have an internal debate. What can you do and what must you do to put it right? Just imagine the results and the whole new love affair with your partner in life, it's really worth the effort.

Make up your mind to take the first small steps towards making your partner feel like a princess, in turn she will make you feel like a prince again. The effect will be overwhelming.

Make a pact to work on this, make it happen. Read this chapter out loud and meditate together.

Follow the rules in the codes of life, this will change your life forever.

A bride and a groom
bind their Souls into one
A partnership, a friendship
second to none
Always remember to drive out strife
through understanding and caring
for your special wife
Continue the courting,
never leave any doubt,
she is the one that your life is about
So care and nurture this for
the rest of your life

Eliyahu Kelman

Chapter Seventeen

Dealing with relationships

- *A revelation going to the very heart of relationships within the family – tackling the in-law and out-law syndrome*

Well, it should have been obvious in the previous chapters that you need to really work to learn the lessons 'off-by-heart'. This does require a lot of effort, and I'm sure that you shared this with those friends who are close to you in order to help them to understand, it does work both ways. The beauty of the Handbook series is the more you share with other people, the more effective it will be. This way you will discover each other. Your relationships will grow stronger, deeper and better. You will start to understand why people can be both negative towards someone, seemingly for no logical reason, and they can be very positive about someone else.

Now, I want to talk to you about children and their relationships with parents, grandparents and family, as well as parents and grandparents relationships with their children. There is a tendency to forget that children, too, have Souls, that children too are sensitive and that children really should be your friends.

They have a need for you to give them the feeling that while you might not like what they do sometimes, that does not mean that you don't still love them. They need to know the reason why you do what you do is that you love them. They need to understand that saying no sometimes shows that you really care about their welfare. Be open and explain that everything you do in this relationship has a reason. Share it with them.

In everything you do, and with whoever you are dealing, even with your children, you should be working very, very hard, together with them, to get up to the Divine Mode and stay there.

We have to understand that in dealing with our children we are setting up their personality for the future. We must guard and nurture their self-esteem, their confidence and how they **Stand-Up** to the many temptations out there.

I received a letter the other day from somebody who corresponds with me quite regularly. A student, one of my friends, in fact, all the thousands of people that I correspond with, I always call them friends, otherwise why correspond with them? We should be interested. Anyway, he related that he was once an alcoholic. His problem with alcohol had lasted 30 years and as he told me, 'I know where the root cause lies; it's because of my reaction to my parents and to my whole environment.

I turned to drink in order to find rest and comfort, and live in a different world. The more I drank, the more I needed to drink. I had an instance in my life where suddenly I felt it was worthwhile to stop drinking. I had a girlfriend who was very, very close and dear to me. She had to deal with my drunkenness and live with it day in and day out.

One day she sat down with me and said, 'I cannot handle this any longer. It is too much for me to watch you destroy yourself. You know I love you very much. I would even like to get married to you, but my parents never drank. I never touched alcohol. I can't stand it anymore. It is against my principles in life and I don't want it. So, I am leaving you, but because you are so dear to me, I am leaving you with this thought'.

His girlfriend went on to tell him, 'I will go away for a month and then you can call me. If you tell me that you are off drinking, I will say, 'Okay, let's go out on a date'. Then we will wait another month and if you have held out and not gone back to drink, we will go out again. We will have a date once a month. If you can keep it up for five years that will prove to me that you have managed to break the habit. If you can show me that you have the will power to bring yourself back to normal, then it will show me that you really care about me and it was worth your while to make that effort'.

He told me that he had not been drinking for eight years since his girlfriend spoke to him. He said, 'I feel that I am able and have the will power to make it up to the Divine Mode now'. He had kept focussed throughout the years because there was a goal and he had achieved that goal.

I wrote back with the following thought that I downloaded from the Big Brain. I was quite pleased because I heard it for the first time as I wrote it. 'Have you noticed the similarity between Spirit and Spiritual? Spirits are alcoholic drinks that cause you to become attached to the bottle, whilst spiritual means you are attached to the Divine Mode.

Every human being has the need to be attached to something! So why don't you simply go out and get drunk with the Divine Mode…, while thinking of the pleasures in life, and those you could be in danger of losing.

We are really talking about relationships. What about our children? After all, he was somebody's son. His family gave him such a hard time because they cared for him, although he never felt that they loved him enough.

They didn't want to go away because they cared enough to say no, and in his particular case, his girlfriend cared enough to say, 'You want to win me over? Then, not don't just woo me, but really win me'. And that's what you have to do.

I learned a very strong lesson about what happens to teenagers when their families either don't understand their needs, or just don't care. People tend to forget what the inner secret of your relationship is with your children, at any age.

Always be mindful of what you say
With words we can hurt,
we can kill and we can destroy
The costs can be high
Beware! you may be
putting your relationships
on the line

Get angry with them,
but don't shout at them
Don't hit them or discipline them
Let them choose their own punishment,
they're usually tougher than you
Always show them that you love them
and are crazy about them!
Tell them that you don't like
what they do,
you just want them
to pull their act together

Eliyahu Kelman

There was something I liked to do with my little kids. I used to say to them, 'Oh, you have got Murphy around you!' I would explain to everybody in the family what Murphy meant. I would say, 'Listen, do me a favour. Go outside. Get rid of Murphy, and when you see that lovely daughter I have, send her inside and you stay outside with Murphy. Sure it was a game! But it always worked. She would go out and after about five minutes she would come in and say, 'I told her to go away and now I'm back in! I'm so happy that I'm going to make you happy'. It worked every time. You turn it into a game.

Don't always take their faults so seriously. This is part of the growing up process. Parents have to keep in mind that each of their children is a unique individual, and must be treated as such. You cannot just take them as a group, a family, school or otherwise and treat them exactly the same; each child will have a different understanding, level of intelligence, home background or experience. Each and every child needs a different set of inputs from their teachers.

Don't always blame the child! When I say a child, I'm talking about all the way till the age of 18 or 20 years old, because they are still your children no matter their age.

Sometimes the fault can lie with the education system or the other people who are educating and guiding them. Always analyse the entire picture, before putting the blame on the child.

Every week we phone each of our children, grandchildren, and even great-grandchildren, thank G-d I have a lot of them. I let them talk and tell me of their experiences and the challenges they had during that week. I just let them talk, a very small part of the conversation is giving them advice on what to do, bringing out the seed that they have in their minds. The secret is to listen to everything they have to say, and act as if you are in their generation.

Sometimes a child will get angry and slam the door, lock themselves in the room or won't join you for a meal. Do you know why? He feels you don't care! And it is generally because of how you reacted to the way they behaved and because you didn't find out what caused it. So, whenever you see a child get out of hand, take the child, sit them down, and ask, 'What have you got to tell me?' Then listen, because that is half the secret of bringing them up. That and making them feel good about themselves.

I have a friend who is a very charitable man. He spends a lot of time and money helping other people, as part of which he runs and funds two major charity projects.

One of them is the popular Big Brother program. He goes to schools and offers a Big Brother companion to any child that is not participating, advancing or keeping up to the standard of their class. The Big Brother comes in the form of a volunteer, male or female, who guides and helps the child with whatever they are struggling.

He now works with thousands of children in this program. It saves them in school, because the teacher doesn't always have enough time to spend on each and every child and the parents are often too busy, working or moving forward with their own careers. They are usually completely overwhelmed and do not know how to handle their children's problems. The project drives him towards helping those that have been neglected and have never enjoyed the advantages of his Big Brother program.

Three times a week, he spends most of the night in the pubs where teenagers go. He took me once to see what he does and it is absolutely overwhelming and fascinating. He actually goes from table to table, sits down and talks to them.

He asks them directly, 'What do you do? What do you feel? Why aren't you home? What's going on?' And then he lets them pour their hearts out to him.

They are generally in the pub because there they meet other friends there who have the same complaints and similar problems. They can cry on each other's shoulders and try to give each other peer support. Every single one of them comes from homes that are in some way broken, where nobody has time or is interested enough to take care of them. They are out of the school system because the school doesn't know how to deal with them. That's what gave him the idea of the Big Brother program and he extends it to them as well. He gives them a Big Brother to act as their friend and guide. In order to put this into 'action', he created a series of homes, which he partly pays for, along with the municipality.

In these homes they receive a lot of warmth, love and caring. They can get a hot meal, a bath, a comfortable bed, a home-from-home, not a dormitory. Each home has a house mother and father on duty to give them what they need.

What have you learned from this?

Now, we are ready to meditate on these thoughts. You must spend time on it and after doing it once yourself, have your children and your wife do it together with you, then listen to this. Don't be ashamed of it!

Let your child tell you where he or she is coming from, because you need to know. That is the only way to do this – together! That is the only way our Handbook works.

If each and everyone treats their family and friends as they do their possessions, their car, their phone, their iPad… Then relationships would thrive.

Whilst meditating, think of each member of your family. Think of your parents and the way you lived your life Try to think what happened to you when your parents 'blew it' or missed out. Think about when your parents did the right thing and you felt loved. Those are the good things that you must repeat in your life with your children… What about the bad things? Cut them out!, your children will appreciate that. Don't be ashamed. Tell them when you have made a mistake with them. Make them aware and share your reasons. Think of all the good things your family have done. Think of all the good things that other families have done and make up your mind to do exactly that with the next generation, because it can only be good. It will help us to live in a much, much better world.

This way it is possible to get rid of the Brain-Pollution, which stops you from climbing up to the Divine Mode. You can never climb up by yourself. You have to do it with your family and close friends. Otherwise, they won't understand and there will be conflicts along the way.

Spaced-Repetition strengthens
the 'learning-curve'
and weakens the 'forgetting-curve'

Science has shown that
when your brain initially puts
information into long-term memory,
you need to revisit it a few times
so increasing the chances that you will later
be able to find it when you need it

Based on the
'Forgetting-Curve'.
an idea first postulated
by Hermann Ebbinghaus

Chapter Eighteen

'The End of the Beginning, a time for reflection'

- *A very personal story showing how any partner or spouse should handle temptations at work – following the codes safeguarding long term relationships.*

Well, we have reached the End of the Beginning. It has been an incredible journey, our first voyage together! We went through a lot. We learned a lot. We discovered a lot and we downloaded software that we never knew was there. Hopefully you have repeated the meditations and self-hypnoses again and again, finding that the more you did, the more it became part of you. The more you are affected by **Spaced-Repetition** the easier it will be to bring on osmosis, triggering off sudden changes in your life, by just repeating it again and again.

Many people learn by repetition. Even fighter pilots learn to fly their planes by repeating actions so many times it becomes second nature. Their hand movements and brain literally go onto **automatic mode**, after a time. It is the same with all the habits that we have in our lives, the good and the bad.

We have made a giant step forward towards placing ourselves on the Divine Mode. I am sure you want to be happy and stay there. It's not been easy to Internalize and work on this alone, the only way is through continued **Spaced-Repetition**.

During this time, you will have had friends and family supporting you, even those who were against what you were doing. And we are going to try to find out why.

Remember Murphy? He lurks in every corner of our lives, waiting to catch you out, waiting to circle you back into the space where you were. That is not his purpose in life, of course. We figured out that Murphy has a better way of calling the other Soul that we have. Earlier, I mentioned we all have two Souls? One Soul will be pulling negatively, the other one positively. Well, obviously the negative one is Murphy. Some people call him Satan, others know of him as the Devil. At the end of the day, he is anti-good and he doesn't want us to succeed. Bear in mind that if G-d created the world and created everything in it for the good, then Murphy too has a purpose. Murphy too has a job to do and you know what that is? He is there to really strengthen us in our determination to fight back, as this is the way we will succeed.

You are not going to let anybody come along and say, 'Ah, give up! Give up on your wife or your husband. Give up on the kids. Give up on your studies. You failed already three times and you shouldn't try again'. Would you listen to such advice?

I have some people in my family who took a driving test five times! They started again and again, not stopping until they had finally passed. Some others didn't stop until they got their doctorate, just carried on with determination and belief, knowing that with that belief, they were going to get there.

I am sure there have been many, many people who discouraged you from making a change in your life, to change your job, to go and study, to combine a job with study, to embark on a new career or try a new business venture. There are so many things in your life and everybody has an opinion! Maybe they want you to be a doctor, but you don't want to be a doctor, because if you were a doctor, you would be a very unhappy doctor. There are many people in this world who are actually stuck in a rut and in a space where they don't need to be.

So, you should remember that there is always someone waiting on the corner for you, it raises the question, 'Why do these people do it?'

I have to be fair to these people around us. Many will give you support. A lot of their ideas are great, and you often receive encouragement and help from them. But, there are those who either don't or won't do this.

They may oppose your ideas actively, sometimes even to the extent of forbidding you. Then again, there are those who just try to bring you down.

Ignore all of them because everyone is equal and has the same chance to succeed on the Soul level.

Get close to the positive people in your life and distance yourself from those who are negative. Choose your own life and choose how to live.

Here I am talking about the chaos that Murphy rejoices in, creating mayhem in your and everyone else's lives. With Murphy, on any level you choose, chaos reigns supreme... Take the media, whatever you hear or see... There is so much Brain-Pollution in the air. That is chaos.

Start your life
on a voyage unknown

Full of adventure,
milestones galore

Signposts of choice on the way
Opportunities, Events, Challenges

All hidden messages
from your mentor, your guide

The direction you take,
is for you to decide

Sometimes you hesitate
on your path through life

Waiting for the message
to show you the way

Is it time to move on,
or is it to stay.

Everything that happens
on the search for yourself

At the end of your journey
be sure that you'll meet

The person you should have been...
and the person you are.

At last you have found
what you are all about

You've reached the end of your journey
that's what life is all about

Eliyahu Kelman

Imagine that you are watching a play, just another scene in a saga and that happens to be quite dramatic right now. Everybody is playing a part in it.

That is your life playing out in front of you.

It is important to have a goal and an aim in this play, it's your life. You have to clearly map out a path where you want to go and what you want to be, or at least to search for a program. Just remember that you are watching a play. Sometimes, you are the star! Sometimes, you are at the centre of the stage! Whilst at other times you are just a two-bit player on the side or out waiting in the wing.

It isn't always about you. It is also about them, the other people in the play, in your life. Always remember that other people have their own dreams, their own thoughts and their own wishes, about themselves as well as about you.

In the last chapter, I talked about how a wife should be treated, just like a princess, because she was always treated like a princess and she always dreamed of being a princess, starting at home, when she was a little girl. And that's a lesson to parents and grandparents. Treat your little girl like a princess then keep it up over the years. Later on, when they want to dress up, what are they doing? Most of the time when they are going out to meet other people, they are all dressing as princesses. Everybody is in that royal family, where everyone should be!

When that little girl or grown woman gives up and doesn't play that game anymore, it is the end, they are finished. They haven't got a chance, because people are judged on how they dress. They are judged on how they look and if they are clean, neat, and tidy. So, most girls, who have been brought up like that have self-confidence. Wherever they go, they wouldn't dare have their friends see them in something which is not pretty or nice. And later when that little girl becomes a bride, dressed exactly like a princess in a Cinderella costume she will be very happy. She will look forward to this part, because that is what she always dreamt about as a little girl. But, don't forget, everybody is part of a royal family, because they have a Soul. On that level that is what they are.

You have to treat yourself and other people with respect. Be aware that there are also dangerous people walking around. Let us call them Agents – the secret agents of Murphy. These agents are genuinely bad people, bad because they can even be decisively wicked. We are going to discuss more on these secret bad agents in future books. But think on why there are secret agents? What is their purpose? Why is one side of the world wicked and hard? This is really a fight between the Sons of Light and the Sons of Darkness, but again, that is on much higher spiritual plain, inner secrets of this world, which are very important to know. Especially for those who have a responsibility towards others.

Does it seem like I am nagging? Summing up the lessons in a different way? Well, you are right. The purpose is to help you to **Self-Hypnotise** and internalise. This is what **Spaced-Repetition** is all about.

Let's get back to the reality of our relationships within our inner circle. First of all, and naturally if you are young, not yet married or don't yet have a life companion, then your inner circle is your parents; your mother, your father, your siblings, and also your friends, I'm referring only to your close friends talking here about only your close friends. They are the centre of your life.

They mean everything to you. If you are married or already have a life partner, then they are the centre of your life, first and foremost. Your family and your life partner's family are second in place. Your wife first and then your children should follow.

The circles that surround you are ever expanding. Life can be a challenge when it comes to in-laws. The world is divided between in-laws and outlaws (and I joke). In-laws are not blood family, but they can be part of your inner circle. You need to make them a part of your inner circle, for the sake of your relationship with your partner.

An important rule to always remember is that when anybody is unhappy or angry with you, has a difference of opinion or an argument, is depressed, or something else has happened to them. It has nothing to do with you. You need to sit down and talk it through.

I have a rule in life – coming from a very strong and powerful secret, going back thousands of years. Never go to sleep with a problem in the air, because we are all Souls and Souls have to breathe in pure air, love, harmony and togetherness.

Don't forget that:

Families, who Breathe Together,
Bond Together and Stay Together

And those who don't, just simply part company. Some people even get very ill or become depressed, because they are not breathing together with their families. So, if this happens, what should you be doing about it?

First, work hard on making sure that the rot doesn't set in. Don't go to bed. Cancel appointments. Give up on that football match. Give up on things that seem important at the time and rather put the needs of someone in your inner circle first. You need to put everything aside, sit down and hear them out. Make sure that you sort it out before you go to bed.

The other night, I saw a look on my wife's face. She wasn't happy and was concerned about something. It didn't matter what it was, I needed to deal with it without delay...

Never let things fester overnight, treat your wife's feelings with respect...

Remember,

She sees the world through her eyes and through her mind

Always Respect that

So I started: '….., we are going to have a cup of coffee and talk it through'.

This sort of thing often happens in our lives, the secret is that you must handle it immediately, never let it fester overnight.

Thank G-d, we have now been happily married for 54 years, partially by sticking to that rule.

I was not concerned that I had important work to prepare that night. I knew that I was filming the next chapters for the up-coming second book, and I had to be somewhere important early in the morning. But, it didn't matter.

It was around half past 11 when we sat down, and it took until 2:30.

My wife is very used to sessions like these and forces herself to stay awake. We go through many cups of tea, and I like to eat an ice cream in order to stay awake. It just works for me. I've always been absolutely determined never to go to bed with a problem in my head.

Watch out for boredom,
it's a clear sign that it is time
to change what you do
Your life redefine,
never remain where you are
Seek out and imagine
your new way of life
Think of the possibilities,
dig into your imagination
You will surely find
your real sense of purpose
hidden inside

Eliyahu Kelman

This time, when we had happily finished, I had a phone call with my son in California. He too had a challenge. He was waiting to discuss something with me, and it was urgent. Well, on the west coast it wasn't yet nightfall, but I didn't want him to go to bed with those worries still in his head. I called him at half past two, finishing only at half past three, then sleeping, ready and awake again at half past five.

Just remember the Rule:

If you are happy,
You're wide awake!
The adrenaline is pumping!
Maybe you'll have to take
another cup of coffee
or an ice cream, as I do,
but if you are happy,
then you won't be tired
You will survive on
the sleep you are given

The truth is personal in everyone's life
The story is always the same,
opportunities, attractions, real life fantasies

We are continuously standing
at the crossroads of our lives,
signposts directing us towards
different destinations;
one pointing towards our home,
our current lives
and the place we chose to be,
the others onto the path
leading into the unknown but
'inevitable consequences'

Stop! Consider which direction is more likely
to bring you peace of mind and happiness
Make your decision before you set out
Just remember that Murphy
lurks in the background
with his tools of trade and entrapment
Walk forward in confidence on the path you
choose towards your own destiny
just reflect and 'muse'

Eliyahu Kelman

Let me end this book with an interesting story before we go on to our meditation. I spoke both in the last chapter and again in this, of Murphy looking around every corner, trying to mess us up, trying to create chaos in our lives, and I have hundreds of stories about him though there is one that stands out. The reason being that it is connected to the subject of the wife and the princess... This is what happened to me.

Many years ago, during the early years of our marriage I enjoyed a very lovely young family and a great wife, we were all very close. We were always with each other, but like everyone else, I had a busy work routine with targets to meet. I had time limitations and the clock governed everything.

Everybody uses the term 'deadline' but I don't like the word deadline, because it leaves you dropping dead at the end of the line. No! It is rather a target. It is something that must be completed, or you have an appointment or presentation for which you have to get ready. And that is what happened to me.

There was a young, very beautiful girl working in my office and she had been chasing me for some time.

Of course, she knew that I was married, but that did not concern her. It was very simple. She had her level of truth and loyalty, and I had mine.

I had a wife and children, who I could never get out of my mind. I was very happy, but at the same time a human being just like everyone else. One afternoon we needed to finish a project that had to be presented the following morning; what do you think happened?

She said to me, 'Look, why don't you come over and have a meal at my house and we can work on it until it's completed?'

My immediate response was, 'What a great idea', knowing full well that I was taking a risk. My wife was quite used to my going out and working at night. She trusted me, but that wasn't the point.

Here was a case of classic Murphy using the most powerful tool he has, 'human-desire'. There is nothing wrong with human-desire, if it is used in the right places and under the right circumstances, but if you are committed to somebody, then Murphy would love to create chaos in your happy married life. He would like to have your wife turn against you, or turn you against yourself.

So, he sends his most powerful tool, which has knocked down many a decent guy or loyal wife. It is dangerous to think that one can **Stand-Up** to such opportunities, when you are clearly being invited. A situation where, seemingly, nobody will ever find out about it, but Murphy knows that if this is a special relationship and it's very attractive, it's like a drug. You will keep going back for more. Then you have choices to make; how many divorces are the inevitable result of things that start like this?

Suddenly the wife doesn't understand you. Why are you so tired? Why don't you function normally? All of the dangerous signals start ringing warning bells and immediately setting off the 'Boom-Box' in her.

I knew why she was inviting me outside work, and I won't lie, I was attracted and tempted. I came home almost determined to go through with it, almost, but I had my moral principles. What did I do with them? I went home. I had a meal with the family.

The kids had eaten early and it was just my wife and I at the dinner table. I looked up at my wife and I looked over at the kids playing nearby. What a lovely gift G-d had given me. Was I going to 'blow it?'

Did I need more than the blessings that I already had? Oh really? Did I? And so I told my wife about the challenge we had and that I had a solution. I told her that we would get a babysitter and that she was going to come with me. I told her to bring a book along, or a few things to repair for the kids but she was definitely coming along with me.

Well, she was of course very pleased but also tickled pink at the idea of her joining us. When the girl opened the door, she had the shock of her life. But what could she do? She had to deal with my wife! I said, 'Come! You have never met my wife and here she is'. So, we had a drink together and my wife said, 'You get on with your work and I will settle down on the couch over here. I won't interfere'.

We worked through whatever we had to complete. Later on when we needed to get a drink, I went and helped her in the kitchen. I was not surprised when she said to me, 'You are an idiot! We had the greatest opportunity! Nobody would have known and I have been wanting for this for ages'.

My response was, 'Trust me, so did I, but I made up my mind that I was not going to let Murphy win'.

She of course didn't understand who Murphy was and I wasn't about to explain it to her. I continued, ignoring her confused face, 'Would I give up my lovely family? No! I wanted you to see what your competition was'.

And it was at that point that Murphy realised that there was no competition. But you know what the real beauty of that instance was that my wife knew anyway; but the extra strengthening of her confidence was important and she felt good about herself.

It actually cured me of the disease. Cured me of the disease, you may ask? Yes, sure, that girl was very attractive, a lot of fun and very beautiful, but I walked away.

Now, you might be in the middle of an affair right now. Walk away. It will be very hard for you to choose, but you see I didn't put myself in the position of 'having to choose'.

This story is very personal, but the truth is, it's personal in everyone's lives at some time or other. But the results depend on what you do with these so-called 'opportunities', at the end of the day we all have to consider the path we choose to take.

Remember that every time this happens, just imagine that you're standing at a crossroads of life, with signs pointing in two different directions, both taking you to inevitable conclusions. One route pointing toward your home, your life, your peace of mind - the other a misty path leading to inevitable consequences. You rarely have the opportunity to backtrack, so aim to make your decisions at a very early stage and to avoid trapping yourself.

Now, this has happened to me a number of times, as new opportunities presented themselves in my life.

The story I just told you applies to every single one of us. Admit it! Either that is what you wanted or the opportunity you found opening in front of you. How many people didn't let Murphy get away with it? So the first thing to understand, if you really want to save your marriage and get close to your family, you must get out of the 'no-good' relationship. The most important thing is first and foremost to be loyal to your inner self.

Yes, first of all, you have to be loyal to yourself. So, if you want happiness and you want harmony, you have to get it on the Divine Mode. You won't get support for anything other than this on the Divine Mode level. Bad situations block the streaming messages.

They close the pipeline to the Divine Mode. They affect everything you are doing.

In fact, you will move the blessings in your life and that is something, which the ancient Sages, right from the beginning of time, warned us against, again and again.

The tendency today is to give the argument. 'Do me a favour. We are living in a different world. There are different opportunities. People don't think that way anymore. Get with the times'. But go and ask your wife how she really feels about your relationship. Will she really have an open mind about it? Just keep remembering - Those Who Breathe Together, Bond Together and Stay Together.

Now, we have to meditate about all of this. It has been a longer chapter than usual, but a very important one for all of us.

We are now ready to go to the next stage and push ourselves up in that beautiful house overlooking the meadow, to see the world from above the tapestry of life. We are ready to remove ourselves from the knots and the chaos of the tapestry.

Think to yourself - do you really want to have the memories of closeness, of happiness, of tranquillity and of bonding together? Do you want to have that feeling, all of the time, that your family and friends are your Soulmates? Well then, close your eyes. Think carefully; close your mind to everything around you and think of each and every member of your family in your mind's eye. Dwell on the meditation with each one and bond with them. Then do the same with each and every one of your friends and then those you are dealing with in your life. Take it step-by-step. It is not going to create sudden changes overnight, but slowly, very slowly, you will see those meaningful changes.

I wish you all the success in the world and all the happiness until we meet again soon. The next book in the series, with the help of G-d will be published during the first half of 1917. It will be full of Secrets, rules and fantastical stories to help us to build more stairs up to the Divine mode.

***Refer to our handbook
for Sources, References,
Bibliographies,
quotes from the Sages and
for more detailed information**

Write to me…

Have a short story?
Tell me all about similar
experiences and messages
that you downloaded
or missed and left you confused.
I would love to hear from you
as I want to get that good feeling
from your wonderful stories,
just like you have experienced
through mine

eliyahu@soulsecret.com

Like a tree in the forest
reaching up to the sky
WALKING TALL
towards our destiny,
not limited by time
Chapter by Chapter together we strive,
climbing mountains to levels Divine,
Internalizing secrets hidden and sublime
Through Spaced-Repetition
repeating again and again
the lessons and secrets,
poems and advice
Stand-Up meditation,
hammered into your brain,
again and again will never suffice,
we pause for a moment with
this book in our hand
Together we stand
at the end
of the beginning
in our voyage through Time

Eliyahu Kelman

REFERENCES AND NOTES

(1) EVERYONE HAS A SOUL

'Anyone who keeps a minimum of the seven commandments of Adam and does not occupy himself with any form of idolatry has a soul' - Talmud Avodah Zarah 3a. Leviticus 18:5.

There is a clear statement in the Midrash Tanah De Bei Eliyahu Ch. 9, and Deut. 13:19

'Bring heaven and earth as my witness whether Jew or Gentile, whether man or woman, whether male or female slave, everything depends on their actions so shall a spirit (soul) of Holiness rest upon them'. In other words 'everyone has The Freedom of Choice' – to choose the path that will take them down to the **Default Mode** or up to the Divine Mode – they receive the 'Spirit level of the Soul which is Ruach'.

Isaiah 42:5; Ecclesiastes 3:19; Maimonides Hilchot Teshuvah; Talmud Sanhedrin 105a; Genesis 2:7; Toseftah Talmud Sanhedrin 13; Talmud Kiddushin 31a; Talmud Chullin 60a; Maharal on Talmud Sanhedrin 91b; Imrei Emet on Parshat Boh; Talmud Gittin 38b; Talmud Kiddushin 41a; Ki Tisah 43 4,5; Zohar 11 94b.

(2) MAN IS LIKENED TO A TREE IN THE FOREST

Talmud Avot 3:22; Deut. 20:19; Orech Chayim 28 4,5; Proverbs 3:18; Jeremiah 17:18 - Mishlei Chet 30.

(3) OPENING THE CHANNELS TO DOWNLOAD MESSAGES.

Psalms 25:14; Samuel 1, 10:6; Samuel 2 23:2; Sefer Yetsirah - Chochmah which is wisdom and the bridge to the level of 'Binah – understanding'. Binah generates the inner thoughts and solutions embedded in any situation.

(4) CHAOS AND BRINGING BACK ORDER TO THE WORLD

The Alshich in his book 'Mishlei Shlomo'. the Proverbs of Solomon. gives an insight into the hidden secrets and rules of this world, also the deep Wisdom of the Bible, and the Wisdom of the Jews. Each Proverb has a significant message for all of mankind on how to live, covering a code of Values, Moral behaviour, human life and the submission to the glory of G-d this is the beginning of all wisdom'. Wisdom is praised for its role in creation and the fight against Chaos which is an integral part of our existence. The practice and awakening of wisdom is the only way to bring back order to the world. Seeking wisdom is the essence and the goal of life on the Divine Mode.

(5) ABOVE TIME SPACE AND MOTION

Zohar 111, 138a, On the Default Mode you are on the level of Malchut – kingship which is material, natural and controlled by the laws of nature. Here we must live in the world of chaos and unpredictability, not so on the DIVINE MODE where there are no limitations or restrictions of nature. This is the level of BINAH – understanding Torah Ohr 152.

(6) THE SOURCE FOR THE NUMBER OF STARS IN THE UNIVERSE

Talmud Brachot 32b. Each of the Zodiac constellations had 30 armies. Each Army had 30 legions. Each Legion had 30 divisions. Each Division had 30 Cohorts. Each Cohort had 30 camps and each camp had 365 myriads of Stars. 12 x 30 x 30 x 30 x 30 x 30 x 365 x 10,000, approximately 10 to the power of 15.

(7) THE BLACK HOLE

Zev ben Shimon - Halevi Kabbalistic Universe & an Introduction to Kabbalah, Samual Weiser Inc.; Zohar 'the creation of the world and the Sod ha Tsimtsum' (the secret of restriction).

(8) THE BOOK OF CREATION - SEFER HAYETSIRAH - ALSO KNOWN AS THE BOOK OF RESTRICTION

This is an important Kabbalistic work, originally written by Abraham - first of the forefathers, tradition has it that the Angel Uziel dictated the hidden secrets revealed within. Rabbi Akivah brought it to life with his clear interpretation of the texts. The deeper secrets of creation are hidden within – the most important being the 32 paths of wisdom. We learn the significance of the word Sefer, a word of three meanings; a book, a Mathematical calculation and a Story. This is exactly how we can learn and understand the Secrets of Wisdom, including those of creation on the lower and higher levels – the Divine Mode and the Default Mode. In addition the nature of space within the human being, creation, the world of the Angels and the Hosts of the Lord. The exact mathematical calculations of the different forms of the 10 Emanations - the Sefirot. It explains the deeper significance of the 22 Hebrew letters, each made up of the three principal letters; Aleph, Mem and Shin. Of these, seven are double-sounding names and twelve are ordinary letters

It is interesting to note that the letter 'Yud'. the smallest letter, is part of all the other letters in the Hebrew alphabet (Author).

(9) I HAVE THE SOURCE CODE

Yerushalmi Sanhedrin 7:13; Tanya, Iggeret Hakodesh 20; Daniel 12:10; Kohelet 9.

(10) EVERY SOUL IS LIKE A UNIVERSE

Baal Hatanyah; Maimonides; Sefer Hayesirah; Sefer Hagilgulim; Baal shem Tov; Rav Nachman mi Breslev.

(11) EVERYONE HAS A SPACE SUIT

'The human body is nothing but the outer garment of the soul'. Zohar 2:76a; Kuzari 3:1.

(12) THE MURPHY COMPLEX – 'DON'T ALLOW YOUR HEART TO FOLLOW YOUR EYES'

Be careful and protect your Soul at all times. Be selective in what you see, watch, look and don't let your heart be influenced by what your eyes can see, It is so easy to fall into a trap'. You have chosen to reach up for the Divine Mode, in order to achieve this, you must never allow yourself to be diverted from your goal in life. Just remember that Murphy is lurking round every corner, waiting to pounce. These are the instructions in Shmah, a special prayer to be read three times a day, to remind us to Internalize and make it part of our way of life. Numbers 16:39.

(13) GETTING UP TO THE DIVINE MODE

'We have in our power the ability to rise to a higher level of Divine attention which is the level of Divine providence'. Ref: Halachic Man p128; Harav J

Soloveitchik; R Bachya in Halachic Man and Chovot Levavot; Moed Katan 28a; Rambam Moreh Nevuchim Vol 111, Ch 17,18; Talmud Yerushalmi Sheviit 9:1; Baal Hatanya on Talmud Chulin 63a; Rabbi Schneur Zalman of Liadi; Sefer Ha Mamarim 5708 p23; Shem mi Shmuel on Parshat Beshalach, Job 31:2; Tanya ch 2; Shulchan Aruch Harav; Orach Chayim 582:7; To quote Chaim Vital on the Ari Hakodesh 'Sefer Gilgulei Neshamot' – 'The Book of Transmigration of Souls':

'In order to help the soul to rise higher in its quest to reach the Divine Mode. As many as eight souls can be introduced at various stages to help, guide and assist'.

(14) ADAM

Every person is referred to as Adam, from the word 'Adamei' – 'I shall resemble the likeness of the Divine. Man was created in his image, after his likeness'. Beshalach 14:21; Shemot 15:16.

The Vilna Gaon teaches an interesting approach to the statement in Genesis 1:26. 'Let us make the human after our image and after our likeness'. The question is asked: who was G-d talking to: The Answer – every living being must work on himself in order to become the image of the Divine on his, her or its level. Perek Shira (See Bibliography p295) was written for that purpose and is songs of praise by the animal, mineral and vegetable existence in this world.

(15) THE BREATH OF LIFE, THE SOUL AND THE POWER OF SPEECH

Genesis 2:7, see Targum Yonatan; Genesis 6:17; 17:15-22; Samuel 22:16; Job 4:9, 27:3; Psalms 18:15; Isaiah 2:22; Lamentations 4:20; Daniel 5:23; Ezekiel 37:5,6,9,10.

(16) THE SMELL TEST

Talmud Sanhedrin 93a, 'Smell is what the Soul benefits from, not the body'; Talmud Brachot 43b.

(17) POINTING A FINGER, COVERS FOUR FINGERS POINTING AT YOURSELF

King Solomon, who had deep insight into the character of man, Proverbs 10:12, 'Love covers all offenses'. a person with many failings will cover up due to self-love. What greater love is there than self-love?'; Leviticus 19:9-18. Rabbi Levi of Berditchev helps us to understand this verse much better, 'whenever you see faults in others, just as you cover up for your faults through self-love, cover up your neighbor's faults' (author: 'and don't point a finger'...).

(18) FREEDOM OF CHOICE

Kohelet 3:11; Devarim 13:15-19; 'I have set before you. Life and goodness; death and evil, you shall choose life'; Deuteronomy 30:15; Maimonides Hilchot Teshuvah 5:3; Yirmiyahu 9:22; Talmud Brachot 33b; Baal Shem Tov; Baal Ha Tanya; Ramchal - Darchei Hashem – The Ways of G-d.

(19a) DOWNLOADING MESSAGES –THE DIVINE MODE TO THE BRAIN

The mortal living on the Default Mode does not see this. 'Mazal, which is his own personal future, potential and destiny' – Talmud Shabat 53b; Talmud Bava Kamah 2b; Zohar 289b. The Chasidic approach is that 'Wisdom can be found from where? From an unfathomable and unreachable place'. The stream of wisdom comes from Levanon - Mazal – Destiny is on the Divine Mode; Megilah 3a; Song of Songs 4:15; Job 28:12, 31:2; Tanyah ch2.

(19b) OPENING THE CHANNELS TO DOWNLOAD MESSAGES.

Psalms 25:14; Samuel 1, 10:6; Samuel 2 23:2; Sefer Yetsirah - Chochmah which is wisdom and the bridge to the level of 'Binah-understanding'. The Binah generates the inner thoughts and solutions embedded in any situation.

(20) THE SOUL - CONNECTION TO A SOULMATE

Genesis 2:18,8; Shaar Hagilgulim; Breshit Rabah 18:3-4; Talmud Sotah 2a; Talmud Sanhedrin 22a; Sefer Ha Chasidim; The Zohar; Baal Hatanyah.

(21) THE OCEANS ARE ENDLESS

Talmud Yebamot 121a.

(22) TWO SOULS (KINGS) FIGHTING FOR CONTROL - THE GOOD AND THE BAD INCLINATION

Tanyah Ch 27; Rav Chayim Vital 'Shaarei Hakedushah' –'The Gates of Holiness'; Ets Chayim Portal 50 Ch2; Talmud Sukkah 22a; Talmud Shabat 152b; Talmud Nedarim 42b.

(23) MAIMONIDES – THE RaMBaM

Moshe ben Maimon (1135-1204). Steeped in the schools of Aristotle, el-Farabi, Avicenna, Avempace – the Talmud and Kabbalah. Famous for his momentous commentaries on all of the important ancient writings. A philosopher and Astronomer as well as a skilled physician, he was born in Cordoba, Spain.

When the Almohads, Berbers and Muslims took away property and wealth protection and gave an ultimatum to the Jews and Christians; either convert, leave or die. As a result he settled in Cordoba, Spain where he wrote Keseph Mishnah, a commentary on the Mishnah. He later moved to Egypt where he was appointed court physician to the Grand Vizier and to the Sultan Saladin. His medical treatises on Asthma, Diabetes, Hepatitis and Pneumonia are still referred to today.

(24) RABBI ELIYAHU ELIEZER DESSLER (1892 – 1953)

Rabbi Dessler came to fame as a rationalist thinker and as source of a book series 'a Letter from Eliyahu'.

He believed that G-d runs everything in this world and can interfere in nature for the sake of man, but that we must make the first move. He should ask for charity, see a doctor, have an operation, go to work and carry on his daily life; with faith and certainty he is helped to achieve what he wants to achieve.

He also believed in relationships between people, nature and society. He is famous for his statement that 'we should always remember that everyone has his or her own level of truth, and we should recognise it as such'. When people do not think or act like us, this does not necessarily mean that they are bad or wrong; their level of truth is different than ours – almost as though they are living in the same world, but on a different plane.

(25) BREAD OF SHAME

Talmud Bava Metsia 38a; the Vilna Gaon and his concept of Nechama Kesufah; Rabbi Dessler; Talmud Orlah 1:61b; Talmud Brachot 48b; Talmud Yomah 38a/b; Yosef Karo on Zohar 2:87a.

(26) RABBI NACHMAN OF BRESLEV (1772-1810)

Born in Poland, he founded the Breslev Chasidic movement which had popular appeal amongst the pheasants and downtrodden, bringing in hundreds of thousands of followers throughout the world.

The movement's big appeal was to call everyone to serve G-d with happiness; there was just no room for negativity, sadness or the like. He insisted that no one should criticise themselves, just search for their own good points and what is special in their lives.

Connection with nature was all important as the Divine is in everything and everyone. The miracle of creation is the binding factor that unites everyone and everything. He used to call on his followers to go out into the forest and talk to G-d, telling him about his dreams, hopes, aspiration, needs and challenges. Again at one with nature therefore at one with the architect of it all.

Rav Nachman was buried in Uman, a city now in the Ukraine – during his lifetime he promised his followers that anyone who visited his grave would receive both his blessing and support for Divine intervention. During the communist era it was dangerous to visit, many of those who did were killed or imprisoned by the KGB.

Nowadays some 25,000 followers celebrate each festival at his graveside.

He was famous for his folk stories about simple peasants and their lives. Each one a parable, the purpose of which was to teach a special lesson in behaviour, way of life, handling challenges, relationships and so on.

These stories were so popular that they were translated into Russian and Chinese by the then communist regimes to show the value of simple peasants and their inner goodness. This of course was to make a negative and critical comparison with all other classes in society.

Some of his quotes were typical of his approach to life.

- 'It is a great Divine instruction to always be happy'.

- 'If you believe that you can damage, then believe that you can fix'.

- 'Worldly desires are like sunbeams in a dark room, they seem solid until you grasp one'.

- 'It is very good to pour out your heart to G-d as you would to a good friend'.

- 'You are never given an obstacle that you cannot overcome'.

- 'The essence of wisdom is to realise how far from wisdom you really are'.

- 'All the world is a narrow bridge, but the main thing is to have no fear at all'.

'As the hand held in front of the eye conceals the greatest mountain, so the little earthly life hides from the glance the normal lights and mysteries of which the world is so full, and he who can draw this away from his eyes, as one draws his hand away beholds the greatest shining light of the inner world'.

(27) HANDLE A PROBLEM IN ITS OWN TIME

'Da tsarah Be-Shaatoh'. The Jerusalem Talmud Masechet Brachot 60b.

(28) THE FINAL OUTCOME IS EMBEDDED IN YOUR FIRST THOUGHTS AND REACTIONS

It's my belief that the poet Rabbi Shlomo Alkabets gave an important message when he composed the now famous poem 'Le Chah Dodi – You are my Beloved'. a song of praise to G-d. He highlighted this secret as a lesson in life. Note: this should not be confused with jumping to conclusions before discovering the truth or an explanation for any event or action (Author).

This is also revealed in the Sefer Yetsirah –'The Book of Creation'. 'The beginning is connected to the end and the end to the beginning'; Psalms 23:12; Nachman mi Breslev; the Zohar; Baal Shem Tov; an example of this can be found in the Talmud Rosh Hashanah 18b and Talmud Baba Metsia 59b.

(29) NO ACCIDENT IS AN ACCIDENT

'Coincidence is G-d's way of reminding us of the existence of an anonymous author'. Albert Einstein and Rabbi Y Schneerson quoting the Baal Shem Tov 'the truth is that there are no accidents, since everything in this world, whether a leaf blowing in the wind or the details of the events in one's life is Divine Providence'; Maimonides commented on Shemot 13:15 – 'Nature is truly all miracles'; Maharal-Gevurot Hashem Intro; Genesis 33:13,14; Harav Soloveitchik – Ber Rabah 39; 'Yetsirah and Assiya - creation, action, a partnership'. 'Nothing is in our hands so leave all foolishness alone, we do not control anything, anything at all'.

(30) KISO, KOSO, KAASO. THROUGH HIS POCKET, WHEN HE IS DRUNK OR ANGRY

In the Book Tanya Rabati, the Maharshah explains that the Talmud, Eruvin 63b, reveals this important secret as the three main character traits for testing and assessing anyone we are dealing with in life.

(31) MENTAL TELEPATHY

There are many examples of this happening in the Bible, the Talmud, the Zohar and practically of the ancient writings. The development of powerful relationships between the Souls. We must work on it

BIBLIOGRAPHIES

ABARBANEL (1437 -1508)

Lived in Portugal, Spain, and Venice. A Minister to the King of Spain and leader of the community. Exiled during the expulsion from Spain in 1492. A key commentator on the Bible.

ARIZAL (1534 – 1572)

Rabbi Yitschak Luria Ashkenasi, known as the Ari Hakadosh; a life cut short, for only a few years revealing himself as perhaps one of the greatest teachers in the world of Kabbalah. Through his leading student Rabbi Chayim Vital, a significant part of His life's work was to bring to life the inner meaning of the Zohar and other ancient texts. His major work on Kavanot, revealing the secrets of the meditations needed to reach the higher levels on the Divine Mode. He revealed the secrets of the souls, reincarnation and identified leading personalities and their Souls' journey from leader to leader throughout history. His main teacher was Elijah the Prophet, who visited the great Kabbalist from the upper levels to teach him all the hidden secrets of existence.

AVRAHAM BEN HARAMBAM (1186 – 1237)

A great scholar in his own right and main disciple of his father the Rambam – Maimonides. Author of Birkat Avraham; Maaseh Nissim; HaMaspik LeOved Hashem.

BAAL SHEM TOV (1700 – 1760)

Harav Yisrael ben Eliezer, known as the Besht – lived in Medzibizh, Ukraine. The founder of the Chasidic movement which spread thought eastern Europe. The special element of love and connection with the peasants and poor folk brought through his teachings and that of his own personal guide, the soul of Achiyah ben Shiloni. At the age of 36 he revealed himself as an important leader and a hidden Kabbalist – He taught the inner meaning of Hashgacha Pratit – Divine Providence, which I have explained in the concepts of 'NO ACCIDENT IS AN ACCIDENT'. EVEN THE IMPOSSIBLE IS POSSIBLE'. 'MESSAGES'. etc.

RABBI CHAYIM VITAL (1543 – 1620)

Chayim ben Yosef Vital was born in Calabra, Italy. Moved to Sefat and lived for some time in Damascus, later becoming the Chief Rabbi of Sefat. A student of Rabbi Moshe Alshich in Halacha and Rabbi Moshe Cordovero in Kabbalah. He later became the closest disciple of the Ari Hakadosh and was appointed to transmit most of most of the teachings of his master, he published Ets Hachayim, Sefer Hagilgulim, Ets HaDaat Tov, the Commentary on the Zohar which was in fact a massive codification of the teachings of the Arizal. Shaar Hahakdamot (the emanation and creation of the world); Shaar Maamarei Rashbi; Shaarei Maamerei Raza on the Talmud; Shaarei Hakavant on prayer meditation; Shaar Hamitsvot – a Kabbalistic explanation of the Commandments; Shaar HaGilgulim and many more covering practically all of the holy writings from ancient times.

THE ChiDaH, RABBI CHAYIM DAVID YOSEF AZULAI (1724 -1806)

He left a heritage in his teachings, revealed in the 71 books he published during his lifetime. A brilliant scholar who wrote his first book at the age of 16. A great Kabbalist and Diplomat who travelled all over Europe and the Middle East, acting as a go-between for the Pasha, the King of Italy and many more.

CHACHAM HAI GAON (939 -1038)

Served as the Gaon of the Talmudical academy in Pumbedita – an institution that existed for over 1000 years. An outstanding scholar who understood, wrote and debated on the Quran and other Islamic writings, familiar with Plato, Aristotle, Alfarabi, Greek history and the Persian language. Muslim commentators even called him the Mutakallam.

IBN EZRA (1089 – 1167)

Rabbi Avraham ben Meier ibn Ezra, Born in Tudello, Navarre, a distinguished poet and philosopher, he created a Landmark Commentary on the Bible and other ancient writings. A master of the Hebrew language and all of its hidden meanings and numerology. He is well known for his poem 'grow old with me'. and 'The best is yet to be' in his philosophical works

288

Browning wrote a poem about him, John Lennon used 'grow old with me'. Isaac Asimov wrote a novel around his personality.

MAHARAL MI PRAGUE (1512 – 1609)

Rav Judah Loewe ben Betsalel, an important Talmudical scholar and mystic. Subject of the famous Golem, which he apparently created as a human like monster using the secrets of the Kaballah to defend the Jewish communities during the pogroms. The good thing was that the Pogromists' really believed this to be true and related many stories that kept them at bay. He wrote many works, including the Gur Ariyeh, a super commentary on the Rashi; Netivot Olam the Pathways of the World, on ethics; Tiferet Yisrael, a philosophical exposition; Gevuroth Hashem – G-d's mighty acts; Netsach Yisrael; Ner Mitsvah; Or Chadash; Beer Hagolah; Chidushei Aggadot and many more.

ORACH CHAYIM (1488 – 1575)

Rav Joseph ben Ephraim Karo famous for his landmark codification and decisions contained in the Shulchan Aruch, for the last 500 years the definitive authority on the laws governing very occasion, decision and action a Jewish individual meets in daily life

Born in Toleda, Spain, he settled in Portugal prior to the expulsion of Jews in 1492. He then emmigrated to the Middle East when the Ottoman Emperor invited the Jews to settle within his Empire. Travelling through Greece he visited with the famous Kabbalist Shlomo Alkabets who revealed that Rav Karo had merited to be instructed by a Maggid - an angelic teacher, he published Beth Yosef on Arbah Turim; Kesef Mishna; Bedek Habayit; Klalei Ha Talmud; Avkat Rachel.

THE BACHYAH, BACHYAH BEN ASHER IBN HALAWAH (1255 – 1340)

A pupil of the Rashbah, the most famous of his writings was Kad HaKemach 'The Receptacle of Flour'. which comprised 60 chapters on philosophy, morality and religion. He is identified as the author of Choshen Mishpat – The Breastplate of Judgment.

RABBEINU TAM (1100 – 1171)

Harav Jacob ben Meir Tam. A leading Tosafist and a Halachik authority, the Grandson of Rashi. Well known for his unique approach regarding Tephilin and his disagreement with Rashi on this matter. Today many people put on both pairs, the Rabbeinu Tam and the Rashi, dividing their morning prayer between the two – the Beinish Chai influenced a whole world of Sephardim and Kabbalists to wear both at the same time. In his public life Rabbeinu Tam was a wealthy financier and a friend of the Governor of the province. Made famous by his book Sefer Hayashar.

RASHI, RABBI SHLOMO ITSCHAKI (1040 – 1105)

A French Rabbinical giant, who wrote massive commentaries on the Torah and the Talmud, a momentous undertaking considering the sheer size of these works. He was known as the Kunterus – The Scribe, because of the copious notes he took at all of his study sessions with the world's famous Rabbis.

MEIER BEN TODROS HALEVI ABULAFIA (1170 -1244)

A major Sephardi Kabbalist and Talmudical scholar. Head of an important Talmudical college in Toleda, Spain. On his father's death he was appointed as the Nasi – known as the prince of the Jewish world. He was in conflict with the Rambam on a number of issues, because of his stature he was able to debate on these questions openly. His commentaries on the Talmud serve as a very valuable guide in unlocking its mysteries. The RaMaH compiled the Orach Chayim, a commentary on the Shulchan Aruch which is accepted as the authority in the Torah world, both Sephardi and Ashkenasi; Darkei Moshe, a commentary on the Tur as well as the Beth Yosef; Torah HaOlah, an in depth philosophical study of the Temple.

RaMaK– MOSES BEN JACOB CORDOVERO (1522 – 1570)

The RaMaK lived in Tsfat, the leading influence in the development of this Kabbalistic city. His knowledge and insight acted as a magnet pulling other Kabbalists to join him in this magnificent centre. Cordevarian Kabbalah centered on the evolving force and effect of the infinite and finite. His encyclopedic work on the Zohar reflected the sequence and logic embedded within. His family originated in Cordoba, Spain – hence the choice of the name. He wrote Pardes Rimonim – the Orchard of Pomegranates, confirming him to be a brilliant Kabbalist and thinker. His major work, written when he was at the height of his reputation and productivity was no doubt 'Ohr Yakar'. the 'Precious Light'. a 16 volume commentary on all of the then known Zoharic literature; Tikunei Zohar is still being published in its new form with 23 volumes produced so far. He continued to publish a whole series of books including Tomer Devorah; Or Neerav; Elimah Rabati; Sefer Gerushin and many more. According to tradition Elijah the prophet revealed himself to the RaMaK, so enabling him to produce the volume of insights that he created in his lifetime. His influence on the great 'lights' of the Kabbalistic world was absolute and supreme.

THE RAMBAN (1194 – 1270)

Rabbi Moses ben Nachman Girondi Bonastruct ca de Porta, known as Nachmanides, born and lived in Catalonia, Spain. A leading Scholar, Philosopher, Physician, Kabbalist and commentator. Starting his writing career at the age of 16 with Milchamot Hashem, 'The wars of the Lord'. His major work was a massive commentary and philosophical comment on the Torah. This was followed by Chidushei HaRamban, an outstanding commentary on the Talmud. He followed with a whole series of books commentating on and explaining a wide range of issues Mishpatei Hacherem; Hilchot haBedikkah; Yavin Hashmuah;Torat HaDam and Shaar Hagvul. Subsequently he delved into calculations on the arrival of the Messiah according to Jewish tradition in Sefer HaGeulah –'The Book of Redemption' - 'Sefer HaKetz'. also known as 'The Book on the End of Days'.

THE RaMCHaL - RABBI MOSHE CHAIM LUZZATO (1707 – 1746)

A prominent Rabbi, Kabbalist and philosopher from Padua, Italy, he spent the last years of his life in the port city of Acre in Israel. Wrote a whole series of Mussar (moral conduct, instruction or discipline) and Kabbalistic books. Mesilat Yesharim – 'The Path of the Just' became the most popular of all, being reprinted hundreds of times in many languages, right up to today. Others include 'Derech Hashem'; 'With an Eye on Eternity'; 'General Principles of Kabbalah'; 'Serving our Creator' and 'The Early History of the Alphabet'.

HARAV SAADYAH GAON (882 – 942)

Rabbi Saadyah ben Yosef Gaon, the first Jewish philosopher to write in Arabic, he lived in Egypt and in Baghdad, Iraq. His first book, 'Emunot VeDeot' was a systematic study, combining certain aspects of Greek and Jewish Philosophy. He descended from the noble family of Judah the son of Jacob, and also the famous scholar Chanina ben Dosa. At the age of 23 he composed a first dictionary in Hebrew 'Agron' which proved to be an important tool for scholars and students at that time. He was appointed as Gaon of Surah the twin academy of Pumbedita; hundreds of thousands if not millions of Talmudical students studied in these Yeshivot for over 1,000 years. He wrote a philosophical study in both Arabic and Hebrew under the titles of 'Emunot ve Deot' –'Beliefs and Knowledge'. in Arabic 'Kitab al Amanat wal letikadat'; 'Kitab al Mabadi'. a commentary on 'Sefer Yetsirah'

– 'The Book of Creation'; Sefer Hahakarah; Sefer Hamoadim and Sefer Ha Giluyim.

Ha RAV DOV BEER OF MEZERITCH (1772 - 1810)

Known as the Maggid of Mezeritch and as Rav Nachman, he was born Dov Beer ben Avraham. His predecessor in the Chasidic movement was this grandfather, Baal Shem Tov. A leading Kabbalist of his time, he re-created the holy brotherhood of the Ari Hakadosh and became the main driver behind the Chasidic movement – teaching love for everyone, calling each his brother. A movement of Song, charity and Understanding reaching out to the masses, the poor and the peasants. He gave practical advice in order to better people's lives, telling stories containing the deepest mysteries of the Torah. The most famous being the stories of 'The Seven Beggars'. 'The Lost Princess' and 'The Master of Prayer'.

BAAL HATANYAH (1745 – 1812)

The Admor Shneur Zalman Borukhovitch, known as Shmul Zalman of Liadia and as the Alter Rebbe. A member of the CHaBaD dynasty, inheriting the title from his predecessor Dov Beer of Messeritch. The Alter Rebbe was the founder of CHaBaD Lubavitch . The incredible heritage he left behind was his special branch of Chasidut, ChaBaD, which stands for Chochmah, Binah and Daat the three important levels of knowledge in Kaballah. Namely 'Wisdom, Understanding and Knowledge'. He was known best for his Shulchan Aruch Harav – the laws and customs according to Chasidut. The TANYA, a monumental philosophical and Mussar work that has been translated into most languages and studied by tens of millions, both Jewish and Non-Jewish, all over the world. He was close contemporary of Baal Shem Tov and Rav Nachman of Mezeritch. His other works were Torah Ohr; Likutei Torah; Sefer HaMaamarim and many more the list goes on and on.

RABBI DOV BEER SCHNEURI (1773 – 1827)

The son of Rabbi Shneur Zalman established the movement in the town of Lyubavichi (Lubavitch), commonly known as the 'Mittler' Rebbe.

THE TSEMECH TSEDEK (1831 – 1866)

Menachem Mendel Schneersohn, the Lubavitcher Rebbe, the third Rebbe of the ChaBaD Dynasty. As with all the important books known to the Jewish World, the Rabbi was known as the Tsemech Tsedek, the title of his main life's work. He wrote a major collection of Halachic law, in addition creating a companion book on the mystical acpects of the commandments, the

'Derech Mitsvotecha'- 'The ways of your commandments'. In his short life he was able to write 'Torah Ohr'; 'Likuttei Torah' in addition to as a well-known philosophical book known as 'Sefer Chakira Derech Emunah' –'The Way of Faith'. He had a close relationship with the personal physician to the Czar, and facilitated delicate negotiations on behalf of the community.

RABBI SHMUEL SCHNEERSOHN (1834-1882)

The seventh and youngest son of Rabbi Menachem Mendel.

RABBI DOV BER SCHNEERSOHN (1860-1920)

Rebbe Shmuel's second son. Commonly referred to as the RaSHaB.

RABBI YOSEF YITSCHAK SCHNEERSOHN (1880-1950)

The only son of Dov Ber succeeded his father as the Rebbe of ChaBaD. He was exiled from Russia after the Bolshevik government attempted to have him executed. He led the movement from Warsaw at the start of world war ll. Fled the Nazis to settle in Brooklyn, New York. Commonly known as the RYaTZ (the previous Rebbe). He established the framework institutions of the CHaBaD movement.

MENDEL MENACHEM SCHNEERSON (1902 - 1994)

Known as Rebbe of the Lubavitch movement and the seventh Rebbe of the ChaBaD Dynasty. He was the pioneer of a massive outreach program, with thousands of Shluchim- Emmisaries sent all over the world where they established CHaBaD centers. There is hardly a city anywhere that does not welcome both travelers and those stranded with love and caring. He was active in helping an untold number of Jews to escape from the Soviet Union and saved thousands after the revolution in Iran. He built up an international network of over 3,000 educational and social centers worldwide, establishing kindergartens, schools, drug rehabilitation centers, care homes for the disabled and synagogues in hundreds of cities in almost every country.

Harav Schneerson's public teachings fill more than 300 volumes. His contribution to a deeper understanding of the Talmud, Halachic and Kabbalistic teachings is far reaching. He published Hayom Yom, an anthology of Chabad customs arranged according to the days of the year. Haggadah in Likutei Taamim and traditions. Over 29 volumes produced from 1952 to 2014. 39 volumes of sichot from 1962 to 1992, and a hundred others – mainly transcripts from his weekly talks.

RaSHBI - RABBI SHIMON BAR YOCHAI (80 – 130)

A second century Tannaitic Sage in ancient Israel, most famous for compiling the Zohar – 'The book of Enlightenment'.

YEHUDAH THE PRINCE (135 – 217)

Known as Rabbeinu Hakadosh –'Our Master the Holy One'. chief Redactor and editor of the Mishnah and a key leader and President of the Jewish community during the Roman era. According to the Talmud he was a direct descendant of King David, recognized as royalty, 'Prince' being appended to his name. The title 'Nasi' was issued by the head of the Sanhedrin – The supreme court of 71 elders.

Yehudah the Prince was born on the same day as Rabbi Akivah met his martyr's death. The Talmud recognized this as the hand of G-d granting the Jewish people a leader to continue the work of Moses and Rabbi Akivah, his father was the powerful sage Rabbi Shimon ben Gamliel. His knowledge of Greek enabled him to act as a go-between to the Roman authorities.

Yehuda the Prince was very wealthy and influential with Rome. Having both a personal relationship with Emperor Antonius Pius and a special friendship with Emperor Marcus Aurelius Antonius, being consulted on many religious and state matters.

SHLAH HAKADOSH (1565 – 1630)

Yishayahu Halevi Horowitz. Known as the holy SHLaH after the name of the book he published. From the tribe of Levi, a scholar and Mekubal, he became head of the court of law in Austria and Rabbi of the community in Frankfurt. He later assumed the position of Chief Rabbi of Prague, the most prestigious position in Europe, even though these communities were opposed to the Chasidic movement of which he was a member. He later moved to Safed, Israel; a city recognised as the world centre of Kabbalah. As a leading figure of the Chasidic movement he would not normally be considered acceptable to the Ashkenazi communities. His concepts of Joy in every action and converting the Evil inclination to the good are the central theme in his Kabbalistic and Halachic works. 'Tefilat HaSHLaH'. a special prayer for the welfare and health of children which had such a powerful effect that is widely used by both Ashkenazi and Sephardi communities worldwide.

BAAL HASULAM (1886 – 1954)

Rabbi Yehudah Leib Ashlag. Brought up as a Porisov and Belz Chasid. Aside from his Opus Magnum, the Sulam (Ladder) explaining the Zohar in Hebrew he wrote one of the most important handbooks of Kabbalah 'Talmud Eser Sephirot'. whilst holding the position of Chief Rabbi of Warsaw he learned German and studied Marx, Hegel, Nietzsche and Schopenhauer in the original. Whilst still in Poland he studied with an unidentified merchant who revealed himself as a Kabbalist. They studied together every night for three months 'until my arrogance separated us'. the teacher disappeared. A few months later he met his teacher again, he begged and finally convinced his teacher to reveal more important Kabbalistic secrets, unfortunately his teacher died the next day. His work is divided into six volumes and sixteen parts, covering over 2,000 pages. His momentous commentary on the 200 volumes of the Kabbalah was almost completed when he died, his disciple and son-in-law added a further three volumes, calling them 'Tikunei Hazohar'.

HARAV MOSHE ALSHICH (1508 – 1593)

Known as the Alshich Hakadosh. Born in the Ottoman empire, he moved to Safed, the world centre for Kabbalah where he was introduced to the secrets and learnings by Rabbi Josheph Caro, in addition he benefited from the wisdom of Rabbi Hayim Vital and Yom Tov Zahalon. Researching by night and lecturing during the day, he belonged to the inner circle of Kabbalists. The name HaKadosh, the Holy One, was reserved to a limited number of Kabbalists, but due to his piety and devotion to his students, together with the deep insight shown in his writings, all of those who associated with him felt deeply that he could not be called anything else. He left behind a rich heritage; 'Torat Moshe'. a commentary on the Torah; 'Marot Hatsobeot'. collected visions of the prophets and their prophecies; 'Romemot El' – 'The Praises of G-d on the book of psalms'; 'Rav Pninim' –'Multitude of Pearls' on the Proverbs; 'Hilchot-Mechokek' –'The Lawgivers Portion'; 'Shoshanat Ha Amakim' –'The Lilies of the valleys on the Songs of Solomon'. presented as a dialogue between G-d and exiled Israel; 'Eney Moshe' – 'The Eyes of Moshe on the book of Ruth'; 'Devarim Nichumim' - on the Lamentations of Jeremiah; 'Devarim Tovim'. –'Good Words on Ecclesiastes'. an interesting concept of deep thought, waters without end and illustration that everything is vanity and having no purpose unless man follows that most essential of his existence –'the love and Awe of the Lord'; 'Massat Moshe' - Moses's Gift, on the book of Esther; 'Havatselet Hasharon' –'Rose of Sharon'. on the book of Daniel; 'Likutey Man' –'The Gatherings of Mannah' on the Haftarot; Yamin Moshe on the 'Masechet Avot'; he also produced a very interesting version of the Haggadah, 'Bet Horin' –'Free Men' - even the Introduction with the laws for Pesach and the order for the evening are treated allegorically and made a vehicle for religious meditation.

SHIMSHON REFAEL HIRSCH (1808 – 1888)

An important leader of the Ashkenazi community in Frankfurt. The publishing of his key works, CHOREV and a commentary on the Bible, have made a major contribution to a number of generations of intellectual youth seeking real answers and guidance within their life and studies. We have quoted him several times in our Soul Secret series

THE RaSHBaH - SHLOMO BEN ADERET (1235 – 1310)

Born in Barcelona, he became a successful banker and leader of the Spanish community. He served as the Chief Rabbi of Barcelona for 50 years. His teachers were the Ramban and Rabeinu Yonah, his numerous students included such famous names as the Ritva and Rabeinu Bachya. His insight and guidance on the Talmud have been studied by millions of scholars and Talmudicals students over the years. He wrote 'Chidushe ha Rashbah'; 'Torat Habayit'; 'Mishmeret Habayit'; 'Shaar Hamayim' and 'Avodat Hakodesh'.

THE RaSHaSH - RIBBI SHLOM MIZRACHI DAYEDI (1720 – 1777)

Shalom Sharabi the Prince, an Israelite Rabbi, Halachist and Kabbalist. The RaSHaSH was born in the Jewish state of Sharab, in Yemen. On his way to Israel he stayed for short periods in India, Baghdad and Damascus, where he was recognized as a great scholar. He belonged to a special Kabbalistic circle of 'friends'. these included HiDaH and Yom Tov Algassi, a devotee of Rabbi Isaac Luria himself, an innovator within the Lurianic Kabbalah. According to legend Elijah the Prophet appeared to him as he was a Gilgul (re-incarnation) of the Ari Hakadosh. The Rashash was a major commentator on the works of the Ari and his siddur (prayer book) was known as the Siddur of Meditations. His writings included 'Emet VeShalom' - Truth and Peace; 'Rechovot Hanahar' - The Streets of the River; 'Derech Shalom' - The Way of Peace. His Responsa to the communities of Yemenite Jews from all over the world was compiled into a series of volumes known as Minhagei HaRaSHaSH'.

THE TALMUD

Otherwise known as the SHAS, it is built around the solid foundation of the MISHNA compiled by Judah the Prince in the year 200, after the destruction of the second temple. The Mishna is really a compendium of all of the Tanaitic writings and the interpretation of the oral law as established by the

Rabbis and the Great Assembly of Scholars, the Tanaim. In the year 500 the Gemarah-Talmud was created through discussions, debate and clarifications by the Rishonim on the writings in the Mishnah. The Gemarah that is studied today was compiled over many centuries of discussion, written in such a way that to the uninformed it seems that great Rabbis, known as Rishonim (the first) and Achronim (the latter Rabbis) were discussing and fiercely debating the possible situations and cases where there legal points with each other and seemingly with people who are no longer alive. Hundreds of Rabbis continued this debate using additional commentaries and clarifications of many great scholars including the Tossafists, Rashi, Rambam, Ibn Ezra, The Rif the Raavad, thousands of books and manuscripts are extant with deep analysis of the commentators as well. One could fill a series of books with the connecting charts and the monumental research projects. An insight into the sheer volume of what is available to scholars today. I have a digital library of over 550,000 source books and manuscripts, and a physical library of more than 5,000.

The range of knowledge and guidance is mind boggling – goes into science, astronomy, astrology, medicine, history, the planet, world and Universe. Two thousand years ago the sages knew about this world – many of which were only revealed or discovered hundreds or thousands of years later. They knew that the world was round and could describe the different nations of the world, otherwise unknown at that time.

The secrets of the world and how the human mind works, advice on marriage, children's education. Life and death, birth, gestation, the next world, mysticism, agriculture and animal husbandry. The sixty-three tractates, 6,200 pages in standard print. Written in Biblical Hebrew and Babylonian Aramaic, versions were created by the Talmudical authorities in both Jerusalem and Babylon, the two versions are studied individually and in groups by at least 1 million people a day, working in multiple languages; by radio, internet, videos, even on the phone. Working at a page a day – an hour a day (each page having two sides, referred to as A and B) takes 7.5 years to complete, the cycle then begins again. Full-time students in Talmudical colleges are able to go much deeper into the texts and commentaries, most scholars focusing on specific Tractates going ever deeper inside.

The Soul Secret Series references a wide range of these sources and their secrets.

THE MISHNAH

Redacted by Judah the Prince – Yehuda Hanasi in the year 200, some 130 years after the destruction of the Second Temple.

The inner meaning of the word 'Mishna' is 'study by repetition'. The Mishna is made up of 6 Orders and 63 Tractates. The Oral law is embedded in the written Torah (The Bible) and recorded in the Mishnah. The 40 years in the wilderness was really an ongoing Talmudical College experience for the entire Israelite population, a full time study of the inner meanings and laws handed down by Moses at Sinai.

THE TORAH

The Pentateuch, known as The Five Books of Moses – The Torah is divided into 24 individual books and has always been the center and foundation of the Jewish people. As an onion is peeled layer-by-layer, revealing so many secrets embedded within. The Bible is timeless, the Bible Codes reveal that future history was written down, in the very finest detail, thousands of years ago right up the current day and age. It is the final authority for everything in everyone's daily lives. The Mishna, Talmud and all the authorative books and manuscripts, including those of the Kabbalah world, are built on this foundation and structured within this edifice. The very blue print for creation, history and the reason for living.

For modern-day scientific scholars there is room for everyone, including for the many creations prior to this creation as recorded in the Bible. Both G-d and history extends into infinity – every letter has its own importance and numerical value, this is used in the system of Gematriah and the deep hidden secrets embedded within.

EIN YAACOV

A compilation of all the Aggadic literature found in the Talmud. Compiled by Jacob ibn Habib and completed by his son Levi ibn Habib after his death.

KABBALAH

Kabbalah – 'received tradition'. This is an esoteric method of discipline and school of thought. All of the books are written in complicated code – even the English translations being too complicated for the uninitiated to clearly understand. The system and method is based on the Torah and other traditional writings.

All Kabbalistic texts are structured around the four principles.

1. PESHAT – the direct meaning of the text.

2. REMEZ the allegoric meaning through allusion.

298

3. DERASH – to inquire, seek and explain the inner meanings of the text.

4. SOD – secret – the hidden mystery embedded in the text, the inner metaphysical meanings according to the Kabbalistic traditions.

A full time exponent of these traditions is known as a Mekubal. In fact the Kabbalah is made up of the Hidden and the Revealed. The Hidden may be studied only by the initiated and special circles known as 'Friends'. these people being unique in their physical and spiritual holiness are known as Mekubalim. The revealed Kabbalah makes up parts of the daily prayers, the meditations for those prayers and blessings in addition to many of the commentaries on the Bible and other Holy books.

THE MIDRASH

Stories related by the Rabbis of the Talmud in order to explain the hidden meanings and the way of life taught in the TaNaCH – **T**orah-**N**eviim-**K**etetuvim (The Torah is the Bible, Neviim the Prophets, Ketetuvim the writings). The Midrash is an important educational tool for the masses who could not understand or study the TaNaCH, Talmud and their commentaries. Many stories related in the midrash were created in order to explain difficult passages and unclear rulings.

THE AGGADOT-THE LEGENDS

These are explanations of the non-legal aspects of the classical Rabbinical writings. The compilations of the Aggadot stories are a mixture of history and folklore, anecdotes, moral and practical advice in all spheres of everyday life, business, relationships and medicine. There are many compilations of the recorded Aggadot. We can find these in the Ein Yaakov; Sefer HaAggadot and other Kabbalistic writings. This is a favorite tool used by all branches of the Chasidic movement.

OR HACHAYIM – THE LIGHT OF LIFE

The Kabbalist Chayim ben Moshe ibn Attar (Morocco 1696 - Jerusalem 1743). This book is a massive Kabbalistic commentary on the TaNaCH. There are other books written by the Ohr HaChayim; 'Hafets Hashem'; 'Desire G-d'; 'Pri Toar' –'A Beautiful Fruit'.

THE PSALMS

Known as Tehilim, the first book in the third section of the TaNaCH. This book is an anthology of psalms compiled and written by King David. The songs of praise take King David through the situations and challenges in his life, the future of the Jewish people, and indeed of the whole world. Each of the psalms have both a prayer and healing significance, a powerful tool in calming down any situation, just read them; the insights are brilliant and very deep.

THE ZOHAR - THE SPLENDOR, THE RADIANCE

This is foundational work of Kabbalah and the handbook used by every Kabbalist. This is the mystical interpretation of the five books of Moses, the powerful weight of the hidden truths can be translated into everyday lives. The hidden secrets, psychology, the Creation of the Universe on all of the levels of man, the Heavens, the Angels and the Divine. The origins of the structure of the Universe, the nature of G-d, the relationship of ego to darkness and the hidden 'self' within. The encircling light and the Universal energy. The Zohar was written mostly in Aramaic by one of the key figures and authorities in the Talmud, Harav Shimon Bar Yochai during the 2nd century. Written during the 13 years that he and his son hid in a cave in the mountains of Meron while the Romans tried to hunt them down. Elijah the prophet appeared to them through very strict and almost impossible levels of meditation, he then taught them the secrets of the Zohar.

SEFER HABAHIR – THE BOOK OF BRIGHTNESS

Attributed to the 1st century sage Nehunyah ben Hakanah, this book is also known as the 'Midrash of Nehunyah baal Hakanyah'. who lived at the same time as Yochanan ben Zakai. This book is very significant in the world of Kabbalah and is a written dialogue between students and their master. It is based on the first paragraphs of Bereshit (Genesis), the first book of the Torah and divided into sixty chapters. We learn much about the mystical significance of the shape of the letters, the signs and the vowel points. We learn a lot more about the significance of some of the statements in the 'Sefer Hayetsirah' –'The Book of Creation' attributed to Abraham and the use of sacred names in magic. A common analogy in the book refers to a king, his servants, his daughter and his garden to illustrate the Bahir's hidden meaning. There is a deeper explanation of the Sefirot, through this he explains his idea that the world always existed in thought, which had to be verbalized by the Divine – until the time of creation as recorded in Bereshit (Genesis) was hidden and stored away.

This book introduced the idea of the reason for re-incarnation where the wicked today are being rewarded for past good deeds with accumulated credits, whilst the just are suffering now for past injustices. Justice is supreme and there is a reason for everything – he called this process Tikkun – a fixing and purification of the Soul; this does not mean that suffering or success is pre-ordained. Every Soul is able to correct their faults and work to rise up to the Divine Mode. Everyone has a freedom of choice and is able to correct imbalances in life.

MISHLEI SHLOMO - THE PROVERBS OF SOLOMON

The Book of Proverbs is the second book of the third section of the Tenach, the 'Writings'. This is not just a collection of advice on how to handle all aspects of life, which has a much a significance today as when it was written, several thousand years ago. Each of the Proverbs give a deep insight into the Secrets and Rules of this world. Each Proverb has a significant message for all mankind; on how to live, a moral and value code governing human life, submission to the glory of G-d - the beginning of all wisdom. This hidden wisdom is praised for its role in creation and in the fight against Chaos, integral to our existence. The practice and awakening of wisdom is the only way to bring back order to the world. Seeking wisdom is the essence and the goal of life on the Divine Mode.

PIRKEI AVOT – THE CHAPTERS OF THE FATHERS

A compilation of the ethical teaching and guidance by the Rabbis for a happy, successful life, including both the dangers and pitfalls. We have quoted extensively from this work.

SHIR HASHIRIM – THE SONG OF SONGS

Also known as the Songs of Solomon, one of the ancient scrolls of the Writings (Ketuvim) in the TaNaCH series. Whilst those who do not really understand the deep significance of this work mistakenly think that this is just a lover's song, it is however a song of love between G-d and the Jewish people. It is a holy book, read every Friday night in Sephardi synagogues and on Passover in every synagogue. As with other Holy Books most of what is written is in code. The Kabbalists have written volumes on these hidden meanings. In the early days of the Soul Secret series we conducted a research encompassing practically all of the source material, creating a new commentary with in excess of 2,000 pages of copious notes. After working for ten years we decided to create the Soul Secret series, a series of books covering the Secrets and Rules we discovered on the way. It has taken another twelve years to actually publish this first book of the series. It is planned, G-d willing, to publish at least ten books in near future. The story is universal, applicable to all mankind, their past, present and future history.

KOHELET

Ecclesiastes, one of the 24 books of the TaNaCH and classified as one of the 'Ketuvim' –'Writings'. classically translated as a Public Teacher or Preacher. The Author introduces himself as the Son of King David, and has been. identified as King Solomon. In this fascinating book he discusses the inner meaning of life and the best way to live.

There are many memorable statements, such as:
- 'Vanity of Vanities, all is Vanity'
- 'We are all limited as humans, why have ego, jealousy, hate, chaos'

After all, everything that is, was and is described in the statement
- 'There is nothing new under the sun'.

King Solomon writes 'When a person dies, whether rich, poor, powerful or downtrodden, the end is the same, they are buried in a field while the living carry on'; 'Life is too short, so why not look for the real values in life and do what we came here for'; 'To build our Souls to do good and be kind to everyone we deal with in life'. As the theme develops he reveals many hidden Secrets and Rules for getting through life and gaining the most by reaching up for the Divine Mode.

SEFER HACHINUCH – THE BOOK OF EDUCATION

This book discusses in great detail the 613 commandments, the book takes us through the Rambam's method of choice as to which commandments fit into the category of the 613 laws as ordained by Moses at Sinai. This is really a companion book to his monumental work, 'The Sefer Hamitsvot' –'The Book of Commandments'. Each commandment being discussed from a legal and moral point of view, and linking to the appropriate source in the TaNaCH, delving into philosophical discussions. This work is used together with many commentaries by later sages such as Rabbeinu Yosef Babad in his 'Minchat Chinuch'.

THE TOSAFOT – THE ADDITIONS

The Rabbis who created the commentaries on the Talmud themselves were known as the Tosafot. Each page of the Talmud as the main text in the center with the Tosafot commentating on one side of the page with the Rashi commentating on the other.. The Beraitot are clarifications and additions external to the Mishnayot. The Rabbis endorsed these Beraitot to clarify points of dissension in real and inner meanings of the Mishna, as additions and an expansion of the Talmud, though sometimes they come head-to-head in arguments with Rashi. The Tosafists lived between the 12th and 15th century, mainly coming from France and Germany, many being students of Rashi himself. The methodology used is a compilation of additions, questions, answers and opinions, only 44 otf the Tosafits being known by name:

1. Avigdor ben Eliyahu Hacohen 2. Asher ben Yichiel (The Rosh)
3. Baruch ben Yitschak 4. Eliezer ben Yehudah of Worms
5. Elchanan ben Yitschak 6. Eliezer ben Joel Halevi 7. Eliezer ben Nathan 8. Eliezer ben Samuel of Metz (The ReEm) 9. Eliezer of Toule
10. Eliezer of Toques 11. Elijah ben Menachem
12. Reb Yitschak - The RiY 13. Isaac ben Avraham - Danpierre
14. Isaac ben Asher Halevi 5. Isaac ben Yaacov HaLavan
16. Isaac ben Meier - The RiVaM 17. Isaac ben Mordechai - The RiBaM 18. Isaac ben Reuven 19. Isaac ben Shmul HaZaken
20. Isaac Di Trani - The RID 21. Israel of Bamberg 22. Judah HaCohen
23. Isaac of Chinon 24. Jacob of Chinon 25. Jacob ben Yitschak Ha-Levi 26. Jacob ben Meier - . Rabbeinu Tam 27 Jechiel ben Yosef
28. Or Jehoseph 29. Joseph Porat 30. Judah ben Isaac
31. Yehudah ben Nathan - The RiBaN 32. Ha Levi
33. Meier ben Isaac (Katzenellenbogen) - The MaHaRaM
34. Meier ben Shmul 35. Moshe ben Yaacov 36. Moshe ben Meier
37. Moshe of Evereux 38. Moshe Taku 38. Moshe ben Eliyahu
39. HaRaV ben Menachem 39. Shimshon ben Avraham
40. Shimshon ben Yitschak 41. Shmul of Evereux
42. Shmul ben Meier - The RaSHBaM
43. Shmul ben Natroni - The RaSHBaT 44. Shmul ben Shlomo
44. Simcha ben Shmul.

MOREH NEVUCHIM - GUIDE FOR THE PREPLEXED

One of the three major works of Maimonides (see page 273). Written in Judaic Arabic during the 12th Century, the equivalent of Yiddish in its relationship to the German Language. This book is introduced as a guide to the secrets hidden within the doctrine of the Holy and ancient writings. He promises the reader to explain the workings and values embedded within the traditions, answering the then conflicts between Religion, Science, Muslim and Greek philosophies, and applying both to his day and ours. It is interesting to note that these questions are eternal and Rambam's guide is as valuable a source for these answers as it was over 800 years ago.

PEREK SHIRAH - THE CHAPTER OF SONG

Moses Joseph De Tirani published Perek Shira with commentaries in 1576, the record however goes back to the 10th century. This beautifully illustrated book is divided into 85 sections, each with a different creature or element of nature, starting with the Divine celestial level and ending with G-d's praises by dogs. The book uses different Rabbinical, Talmudic, Kabbalistic, the Psalms, Book of Maccabees and Torah references in song form, assigning each to a different element of nature; animal, mineral and vegetable. The sage Joseph Albo, advised people to recite this daily in order to gain 'The world to come'. The reason being that we can learn from all of these songs, with one thought in mind, that if nature recognizes the power of the Divine, then mankind and their Souls are at one with everything in the universe. In addition each one of us has a special prayer to recite.

TARGUM YONATAN

Written by the poet and scholar Yonatan ben Uziel, one of the 80 Tannaim who studied under Hillel the Elder. This is the book of the Kabbalah known as Meggadim which is mentioned in the Talmud. The Commentaries are interesting because many times we find that the prophetic insights have been playing out repeatedly over the last 5,000 years.

THE KUZARI - KHAZARS

A famous philosophical book written by the poet and scholar Yehudah Halevi. He was a leading Spanish philosopher and sage who completed the book in 1140, nearly 900 years ago. Known as the Book of the Khazars, it was divided into five sections, playing out a discussion between a Rabbi and a Pagan king, identified as a king of the Khazars, who had invited the Rabbi to explain and discuss the Jewish religion. It is not generally accepted that the kingdom of the Khazars converted to Judaism but there were students who claim that they met Khazar Rabbis in the 12th century. Yehudah Halevi created a dialogue between the King and a Christian followed by a Muslim philosopher. The dialogue takes the discussion towards the conclusion that both religions are rooted in Judaism and that's where the King wanted to be, we used parts of this discussion as source material for revealing some of the Secrets and Rules that apply to all three religions. The King's search followed on from a dream in which he was told that whilst he and his people were good, kind and just, he should seek out a religion that worshiped one G-d and to immediately leave his Pagan ways.

HARAV CHAIM SOLOVEICHIK (1903 – 1993)

Known by all of his followers worldwide as 'The Rav'. He personally ordained over 2,000 Rabbis in his lifetime. Joseph Beer Soloveichik was a direct descendant of the Soloveichik dynasty, going back some 200 years. Talmudist, Scholar, Philosopher and Dean of the Maimonides school at Yeshivah University in the USA. He served as advisor, guide, mentor and as a role model for hundreds of thousands of followers throughout the modern world, and was a pillar of strength both during and after the Holocaust. The most significant presentation of his philosophy was his book 'The Lonely Man of Faith'. the inner conflict between an individual's human existence and his soul. Bringing in the example of Adam, whose birth is mentioned twice in the Bible; one created on earth in the garden of Eden and in the other being created in the Heavens and brought down to the Garden of Eden. We have used this book as a reference for a better understanding of our concept of the Default Mode and the Divine Mode; 'Halachic Man'. 'Halachic Mind'.

THE TEN SEPHIROT – THE TEN EMANATIONS

These Emanations or attributes through which the Divine 'Ein Sof' – 'Without End'. on the Soul level, continuously linking the physical to the spiritual realm - A reference to the concept of the Divine and Default Modes. Sourced in the Zohar, Parshat Chayei Sarah; Sefer Yetsirah and all of the kabbalistic books. There are many different combinations of the Ten Sephirot depending on the subject involved.

Printed in Poland
by Amazon Fulfillment
Poland Sp. z o.o., Wrocław